Gerald Priestland

THE CASE AGAINST GOD

COLLINS
8 Grafton Street, London WI
1984

William Collins Sons & Co. Ltd
London · Glasgow · Sydney · Auckland
Toronto · Johannesburg

BRITISH LIBRARY CATALOGUING IN PUBLICATION DATA

Priestland, Gerald
The case against God.
1. God – Proof
I. Title
212'.1   BT102

© 1984 Gerald Priestland
First published in Great Britain 1984

ISBN 0-00-215142-1

Photoset in Linotron Plantin by
Rowland Phototypesetting Ltd
Bury St Edmunds, Suffolk
Printed and Bound in Great Britain

THE CASE AGAINST GOD

Gerald Priestland is probably best known for his thirty-three years as a BBC correspondent. His posts ranged from 'Today in Parliament' to Delhi, Beirut and Washington, and ultimately Religious Affairs.

His talks 'Yours Faithfully' and 'Priestland's Progress' became national institutions and successful books – as did his recent television series, *Priestland Right and Wrong*.

On retiring from the BBC in 1982 he took up freelance writing and broadcasting.

He was educated at Charterhouse and Oxford, where he was a pupil of Isaiah Berlin and Stuart Hampshire.

Gerald Priestland is married to Sylvia Priestland, the printmaker, has four children and lives in North London and West Cornwall.

With respect, to the Doubtful

Contents

Introduction

A few years ago, in the book and radio series called *Priestland's Progress*, I said that one day I would love to tackle the question of God's existence. This is my attempt.

I have approached it, rather aggressively, as the case *against* God for several reasons but primarily because I think it is the best way of drawing the case *for* Him. I do not want the reader to think, however, that the case has been rigged from the start. I have always been prepared to find myself persuaded that He did *not* exist, and there may be some readers who will conclude that my ultimate stand is not a real conviction at all and that, in fact, I do not believe in the living, full-blooded God they know. The last thing I want or expect to do is to shake their faith: I am sure they are immune to anything I can say.

I am much more concerned with an audience which revealed itself in response to *Priestland's Progress*, composed of people both inside and outside the churches who hope and even trust that there is a God and who feel the power of Jesus but find too much in the traditional protestant and catholic interpretations of the Bible to which they cannot, in good conscience, subscribe. These are honest and valuable people, not to be dismissed as second-class souls, and it is my belief that the acknowledgment of their doubts can only stimulate the churches to develop their faith with still deeper insights into its truth. It is an evasion to say flatly 'The Bible is the Word of God – it is true!', for all religious talk is analogical, poetic, expressionist, open-ended, subject to interpretation and correction.

That applies also to the three inadequate slogans which now encapsulate my faith. The first two evolved during *Priestland's Progress*:

1 If Jesus was not God, He is now.

2 In Jesus, God was saying 'I am like this – and I am so like this that, so far as you are concerned, I *am* this.'

To these paradoxes, as a result of this present enquiry, I have presumed to add:

3 God would not be the God that He is if we could prove that He was.

I am not attempting to nail these to the door as complete, self-evident dogma; but to me there is some life and growth in them. To others they may be sufficient proof that there can be nothing of value in the pages ahead.

My third slogan may also seem to condemn this enquiry into the existence of God to failure in advance. But to me it is the pilgrimage itself which is the purpose, and that pilgrimage includes the struggle in the dark. Two things compelled me to commence this investigation: the story of the trial of God told to me by Rabbi Hugo Gryn, as related in my first chapter, and my rediscovery one day of the legend of Jacob wrestling with the mysterious stranger at the ford. This is commonly described as Jacob wrestling with the angel; but it is quite clear that the stranger was no angel but God Himself. For at the end Jacob declares 'I have seen God face to face and my life is preserved'; and he gives the place a name which means 'the face of God'. What seized me, however, was not the ambition to 'see God face to face' but the very example of Jacob grappling with his mighty antagonist, even beyond the point at which he was crippled by him, and crying 'I will not let thee go, except thou bless me'. I am no Jacob, but his story seemed to tell me that I was not going to find God's blessing unless I dared to wrestle with Him through the night. And again, in the story of Job – an obvious inspiration to this enquiry – I read that even though God's answer might be a dusty one, He required the one who sought him to 'gird up his loins like a man'.

Speaking as if from the far end of this book there is a further good reason for undertaking it, and that is the need to resist the spread of – largely unconscious – atheism in our society. It is not so much that people deliberately renounce God in the way that so many have renounced the churches, but that they cease to behave as if there were a God and seem to regard Him as optional. The result of abandoning the supposed fantasy of God has been a general surrender to the fantasies of politics and economics. As Professor David Jenkins, now Bishop of Durham, once put it: 'Politics is no longer the art of the possible – it has become the pursuit of the fantastical . . . A major source of the pathological dominance of fantasy in our current thinking and actions is the collapse of effective belief in God, and a failure to face up to the practical consequences of atheism.'

I am not arguing for a theocracy; but over the past three centuries humanity has increasingly put itself in the place of God and invested the State with God's divinity. It is the State which is expected to deliver the godlike possibilities which humanity detects in itself. That we have not, even now, seen through this fallacy is due to our devotion to political fantasies beside which the Bodily Assumption of the Virgin looks like a hard fact. What evidence is there that our political leaders have any serious grip on reality? Is there any visible connection between what the party manifestos and conference decisions say and what actually happens? Being fantastical, politics have to be pursued by increasingly irrational and arbitrary methods: facts are no longer neutral, they are good, right and true if they conform to the party fantasy – bad, wrong and false if they do not. And so we sink deeper and deeper into a kind of alternating totalitarianism. (I am much obliged to Professor Jenkins for his righteous indignation about it.)

But this is to put the cart before the horse; or, rather, to assume that there is a horse to pull the cart. My own particular show went on the road in February 1984 when Chris Rees – my producer, as he was for *Priestland's Progress* – our engineer Malcolm Stokes and I set out to conduct more than eighty interviews with people who we thought might have interesting views on God or His nonexistence. In a matter of two months we ranged from Scotland to the West Country – and even further. We did not feel we could limit our search for God to Anglo-Saxon attitudes alone, so we contrived an excursion to Rome, Jerusalem, Cairo and Delhi so that we could collect some evidence from Catholics, Jews, Muslims, Hindus and Buddhists as well, in their own perspectives.

As with my previous radio series I am very grateful to the BBC and its Religious Broadcasting department for these opportunities. I am grateful also to Chris and Malcolm for their companionship as well as their skill; and in this I must include our secretary, Amanda de Winter, who dealt with an enormous volume of paper-work, and Patrick Forbes, our researcher, who was responsible for locating our witnesses and fitting them into a schedule. The fact that we had all worked together successfully before gave me, at any rate, a sense of confidence.

The great majority of our witnesses had not featured in the *Progress*, and the strain of the interviewing lay not so much in the actual questioning before the microphone as in breaking the ice with so many strangers, three or four times a day. In order to make them feel, and sound, at home we conducted all but a handful of the interviews in the witness's own study or sitting-room. I am grateful, again, for so much patience and hospitality (Marghanita Laski gets the prize for the best tea, with the former Archbishop of York as a close runner-up).

Inevitably, only a fraction of what people had to say could be included here, and there was even less room in the radio programmes. Some witnesses must be disappointed to find they make no appearance in either medium. To all, my apologies and my assurance that everyone has contributed something to my education, whether I have seen fit to pass it on to others or not. As I have tried to convey, it is, in the end, the presence and personality of the witness that persuades, far more than what he or she actually says.

Two things in conclusion:

Let me earnestly repeat that I am not seeking to undermine the faith of those who have it. If that faith is real, I cannot.

And I must record my gratitude to my wife Sylvia who once again had to endure the absences, the tantrums and the endless clatter of the typewriter that projects like this inflict on innocent bystanders. I am sure Chris Rees and Patrick Forbes are saying the same to their wives, who have our sympathy.

1

Case for the Prosecution

I have this weakness for rabbis, especially of the Reform
persuasion. In fact I am proud to say that some of my best
friends are Reform rabbis, including Lionel Blue (broadcaster
and cookery correspondent of the Catholic newspaper *The
Universe*) and Hugo Gryn, who supplies me with most of the
religious jokes I know. I think it is this rabbinical passion for
telling stories, rather than embarking on theology, that appeals
to me; for stories are human and seldom dogmatic. They were,
after all, Jesus's favourite form of teaching.

But the story which became the origin of this investigation
was not a particularly funny one. A number of Jewish writers
have recorded it, but Hugo Gryn got it from an uncle of his who
was there in one of the sub-camps of Buchenwald. In this camp
there happened to be a group of particularly learned Jews,
several of them rabbis. They had to work six-and-a-half days a
week, but on Sunday afternoons they were left in relative peace.
One such afternoon the learned Jews, in their despair, took up
the notion of putting God on trial – not so outrageous as it may
seem, for there is a Hebrew term meaning 'to have a legal
disputation with the Lord'. So witnesses came forward for the
prosecution, there were others for the defence, and there was a
bench of rabbis acting as judges.

The case for the prosecution was overwhelming. They had
only to look at their condition. Their community was being
wiped out; most of their families had already been destroyed;
how could a good God permit this to happen? The case having
been made and a desperate defence put up, the judges had little
difficulty in reaching their verdict: the accused was guilty as
charged – guilty of neglecting His chosen people. Silence fell
upon the court, until one elderly inmate rose to his feet.

'Nevertheless', he said, 'let us not forget. It is time for our evening prayers.'

Like all the best stories this one kept coming back into my mind, compelling me to turn it over and over, for there was so much in it. I knew from my correspondence that for many people the greatest single obstacle to faith was the glaring fact of wholly unmerited human suffering; and it was there in the Holocaust on a scale that could not be brushed aside. The best a Christian could do was to talk about mystery and speculate, unconvincingly, about the redemptive power of suffering. But here were pious Jews, who had been abused past endurance, complaining into God's very face, demanding satisfaction, and condemning Him when they failed to get any. What was more, having condemned Him, they worshipped Him. It was power-ful nonsense, glorious misery, the sort of paradox needed to hold great truth.

And so the idea began to grow in me of putting God on trial in the hope of hearing His defence. But as the possible evidence unrolled in my imagination, I could hear learned counsel protesting 'M'lud, this trial is a farce! I submit that the accused simply does not exist. To my clients a verdict of guilty would be as ridiculous as one of not guilty. Either verdict would only serve to perpetuate a fairy tale.'

In all fairness, the charge would have to be amended to one of cruelty, incompetence and possible nonexistence. Even then, counsel for the atheists was far from satisfied. How could the trial be a fair one when one man – of notoriously religious inclinations – proposed to make himself prosecutor, defender, judge and jury, not to mention editor of testimony? It will not quite do to plead economy and practicality. I can only say, in all seriousness, that I find all those roles present within myself, including that of doubter. The court is within me, and some might say that what is really at stake is my own soul. If they are frank with themselves, I think that may be true for a good many of my readers and listeners.

Is there a God? The French philosopher Pascal concluded that belief was the wisest bet because the believer will either have bliss if he is right or oblivion if he is wrong, whereas the unbeliever has the less attractive alternatives of oblivion or

damnation. But this looks morally and intellectually disreputable. It is pretty clear that we cannot stage public demonstrations of the existence of God, as we might of the existence of
gravity, or there would be no argument about it at all. But why
do people *claim* that He exists? What incomplete evidence do
they have towards that claim; and does it at least make Him
more likely rather than less? In any case, what do believers (and
unbelievers) *mean* by God?

A correspondent with the Quaker journal *The Friend* (Mar-
tyn Grubb) recently proposed that the whole discussion of
God's existence was based on a fallacy, since by definition 'God
is the name we give to whatever does exist'. If that really were
so, the debate would indeed be a waste of time: but I do not
think it is so. Most believers make a very clear distinction
between the Creator and His creation, the Redeemer and the
redeemed; and even if we adopt the picture of everything
existing as 'ideas in the mind of God' we are not saying
'everything *is* the mind of God'. It is the very feeling that there is
more to the universe than we can *show* to exist that leads us to
use a term like God at all. And the fact that people have used it
devotedly, persistently, usefully and most of them would say
meaningfully for so long, while it is not proof of His existence in
itself, does at least suggest that we have to take it seriously.

But still, what kind of a God do we have – if He exists – and
what is He doing – if anything? If He exists, and if He possesses
the sort of qualities which believers usually attribute to Him,
like omnipotence, omniscience, omnipresence, perfect goodness, justice and love, then why does He permit atrocities like
the Holocaust to devastate His creation? This is an exercise
usually known as the problem of evil, or theodicy ('justification
of God'), and we cannot very well take up the question of God's
existence unless we are prepared to take up this as well. Very
few believers would be happy to find themselves the children of
an indifferent monster.

This, then, is the sort of intellectual terrain we shall have to
cross if we insist on asking that first question. But of course we
are not obliged to take the challenge. There are some happy
souls who know the answer so clearly that the question asto-

nishes them: like Jane Adams, a young Christian housewife from Slough, who told me:

> I just know that the Lord is real – I feel Him living inside me. I can't really explain, but I believe that Jesus Christ is the Son of God, that He was sent by God, that He's one with God. I believe that He died for us and that He rose again from the dead and that He's alive now today. And I believe that the only way to God is through Jesus Christ and what He taught in the Bible and what's written down for us in the Bible.

And this even though Jane had just lost her four-year-old son because of a heart defect. She felt no bitterness; she was perfectly sure that God was controlling her life and that of her child. Belief of this kind seems quite unshakeable (and one would hardly wish to shake it), but impressive though it is it remains something given, something personal, something that it is impossible to catch by enquiry.

One of the turning-points in the philosophy of religion came with the great Lisbon earthquake of 1755, in which hundreds of people died in church celebrating the Mass. Coinciding as it did with the Age of Reason, it made people ponder the irrational nature of suffering, and question glib theodicies which sought to explain it in terms of God's punishment to the wicked. I think there are better ways now of fitting a good God and unmerited human suffering into the same universe – and we shall come to them in due course – but I do not want to insult the deep feelings of people like Gerry Fitt, or the real indignation of so many nonbelievers, by propounding them instantly. One of the most impressive of contemporary liberal British theologians is Frances Young, of Birmingham University, who finds herself most unhappy with Christian efforts to explain away suffering. Too often, she thinks, they become philosophical attempts to cover all eventualities; and, worst of all, they fail to take account of what lies at the heart of the Christian religion, namely the Cross – the paradigm case of the suffering of the totally innocent.

True, that could be seen as a revelation of the ultimate wickedness of humanity – not of God. But Frances Young was not inclined to use the resurrection as a magic wand to make all well again (as some Christians are inclined to do). We had to take very seriously the extraordinary picture that the gospels in no way gloss over, of Jesus plumbing the very depths of suffering to the point of abandonment by God:

> I think there is something in everybody who faces suffering which leads them, if they believe in God, either to question His existence or doubt His goodness and to blame Him; and I think it is right and proper that people should face that. I think there is too much tendency to sweep suffering and evil under the carpet with glib explanations and not face the depths of what it actually means to go through the black hole and not be able to understand. I think the kind of protest and even blasphemy found in something like the Book of Job is very important, and people who give glib answers to the problem of suffering probably haven't ever looked into the depths. We just have to face the fact that there are times when protest and blaming God is appropriate. It is part of the human condition, and if we can get down on our knees and voice our protests we're being honest. And the most important thing before God is to be honest.

In Frances Young's own experience, the black hole may actually lead to the presence of God, 'a kind of resurrection experience which can transform the situation in a profound way, and almost justifies what has gone before . . . It's very often in those deepest moments of darkness that people do actually sense the presence of God. It's not when everything is going smoothly.'

But I am writing as if we were certain of God; and if we are to be honest we must accept the honesty of those who deny Him. At the same time, from the very start, we have to be sensitive to a tricky distinction: between God Himself and what is said and done in His name. Unbelievers may well groan at this, anticipating a constant stream of: 'but God isn't really like that – that's a misunderstanding we've now corrected'. Nevertheless, if there is a God and He is palpably not riding round the universe in a fiery chariot making personal appearances, He could only operate through human and natural instruments and the former, at any rate, have never pretended to know exactly what it is He wants. In other words, while the atheist may have come to the end of his road, the believer is well aware that his own will never end.

In this spirit, Professor John Bowker, of Lancaster University, while very much a believer, welcomes a great deal of modern scepticism as a sign that our traditional images of God have collapsed as inadequate, and that every protest against His character and the enormities that have been done in His name must be taken positively. It is wrong, he thinks, to respond to every criticism by looking for arguments against it. Atheism should be seen as an opportunity to learn and be humble. John Bowker went on:

> The protest against God is not just occurring within Christianity, so you can't just tie it to the Church. I attach much more importance to the unease about what has been claimed about God, and the lies that have been constructed from the resource referred to as God. I take most seriously two protests. The first is the irrelevance of God: what possible difference could God make in the sort of universe we now imagine. The second is that really heartfelt cry of anger and anguish about what has been done in the name of God. I think that's very much stronger than the traditional problem of why there is so much waste and suffering, which doesn't bother me at all as an intellectual problem – though it does as a matter of friendship and compassion.

How Bowker copes with the intellectual problem of suffering, we shall see later. A fine example of protest against what has been constructed from the 'God resource' came from the philosopher Sir Alfred Ayer, a dedicated atheist, though he admits to being intrigued by the Jesuits. Said Sir Alfred:

> I am very hostile to Christianity because I think it is a wicked religion. I think Christianity is based on the notion of vicarious atonement which shocks me not only intellectually but morally. If I have one child, I don't punish his brother for what he did – and that is exactly what Christ-

ianity is based on. There is a deity who created a certain set
of people with certain appetites (these stories are so ridiculous, anyway) and then, when they behaved in a way He
didn't approve of (and what He did approve of was pretty
horrific) the Jews were massacred and generally de-
frauded. Nobody reads the Bible. Indeed, the savagery of
the New Testament is also overlooked. Here you have
your deity who did all this. And then He said suddenly:
'People are behaving badly. I am going to transform
myself into a human being and suffer vicariously. Sins
have to be atoned for by a sacrificial lamb.' So Christ is
supposed to atone for the sins that other people committed. The whole thing is not only intellectually contempti-
ble but thoroughly outrageous.

When I suggested that a good many Christians no longer saw
the cross like that, Sir Alfred retorted that Oxford college
chaplains did not seem to believe in anything at all; except,
perhaps, good works among the poor in the East End of London.
Personally, he had begun to lose his faith when he prayed to get
into the school cricket team and had his prayer rejected.

Professor Ayer's mother was Jewish, and there is a Jewish
background to one of my most engaging atheists, Jonathan
Miller, whom, I suppose, I might describe as anything from a
medical man to a producer of operas. By accident, I met him
first at the Wailing Wall in Jerusalem, staring in amazement at
the pious bobbing and bowing and inveighing against the God
who demanded it, sentiments he recalled when we met again at
his house in London:

> Yes, on the whole I've always been annoyed by the Jewish
> God. I think he's authoritarian, vindictive, capricious,
> spiteful and, worst of all, absent most of the time. And
> then he goes into these hideous tantrums on his return,
> like some awful Jewish father that leaves the house, ex-
> pects good conduct, and then on his unexpected return
> smashes the furniture if people have been behaving badly.
> So I don't on the whole like the monotheistic Jewish God.

Miller thought the Christian God was something of an im-
provement. The Incarnation was 'quite a brilliant invention

and, let me hasten to add, Jewish. One of the great mistakes of
the Jews was to let go of the franchise on it.' But he still could
not approve of the Christian relationship between Creator and
creature:

> I really hate the idea of a God who gives human beings free
> will in order for them to choose whether they are going to
> be sinful, in order to have to offer redemption, in order to
> avoid punishment. It is as if God was running a gigantic
> Wosbee – one of those War Officers' Selection Boards –
> and He calls everyone in: 'Make yourselves at home in this
> country house I'm running. It's going to be quite an
> interesting affair – one or two obstacle courses – some
> people will come unstuck here and there – but I can assure
> you that it's going to be quite an interesting choice when it
> finally comes to it; and I think I'm free to tell you that some
> of you are going to rise to Field Marshal . . .' If God is like
> that, He ought to be ashamed of Himself – and for all the
> things He has visited upon His creatures and makes His
> creatures visit upon each other – perhaps those are the
> worst ordeals. Earthquakes I can put up with. Pillars of
> salt – fine. Inundations – perfectly reasonable. They're all
> dealt with in the clauses of insurance contracts. What I
> think is unsufferable on the part of God – if in fact there is a
> God – is to have invented a creature who visits more
> suffering upon himself than inanimate nature can inflict.
> That, I think, is something for which God should be at
> Nuremberg.

Jonathan Miller is one of those rare figures who claims never
to have had any kind of belief at all, never to have had a childish
faith which he lost. He is the complete agnostic, not in the sense
that he is waiting for further evidence that might convince him,
but that: 'I haven't the faintest idea of what people are talking
about. I don't know what the question means. I can't get my
head round the concept of God and I certainly can't believe in
him in the way He is currently described by most religions.' As
we shall see, Miller is sometimes moved by the spectacle of
belief in others. But he is – justifiably, in my view – exasperated
by those who try to convince him he is 'really on the road to

faith'. It is impossible to prevent a believer from seeing God, or God's purposes, in an atheist: I think, myself, that the atheist is necessary to our apprehension of how God is. But it seems to me unforgivable to try to push the unbeliever into redefining himself as a believer.

John Mortimer, barrister and playwright, was another engaging witness of this type. As a newspaper interviewer he constantly asks people about their belief, because he thinks it 'defines a person very clearly'. But:

> I can't accept the idea of an omnipotent creator who allows the gassing of seven million Jews, or children dying of leukemia, or the horrors that are going on in Cambodia and South America. I can't find his excuse for that. Either he is not omnipotent or he fails to stop it for some theoretical reason of his own, which I find difficult to accept. I don't understand why he created a world in which all that suffering was a part, unless he had some reason. And the reason which appears from any interpretation of Christianity is that in some way suffering is good for us. And I think this leads to the ill-effects which I think Christianity has had: that it becomes a religion of suffering, in which what happens in this world isn't important compared to what is going to happen to us in the next. It becomes a religion in which people can be reconciled to their poverty and their ill-health and their lot in this world, without people having to bother to rectify it.

John Mortimer has had plenty of opportunities, as an interviewer, to worry this out with the highest in the churches. But they have given him little satisfaction:

> I asked Cardinal Hume what he thought about leukemia and concentration camps, and he added the example of children crushed to death in crowds that go to see the Pope. And he said he couldn't ask those questions as if he and God were on the same level. But as a barrister cross-examining a witness, I have got to assume that we are. So the outcome of Cardinal Hume's theories on the matter was that it was a mystery. I asked Archbishop Runcie of Canterbury what he thought about it; and he

said he was an agnostic so far as God's purposes were concerned – he didn't really answer the question. So from neither of these did I get a very clear answer, and it seems that on this vital issue Christianity is silent. I find it very difficult to live with a religion that does not answer that question itself.

Mortimer has a further, personal, difficulty about accepting the notion of God. He is intensely allergic, he says, to judges; and cannot bear the idea of God as the senior judge in the Court of Appeal, before whom we shall finally appear. What he would like to think is that there is some quality in every moment of life 'which transcends its more mundane aspects – which suffuses it with some great importance'. But he does not think that means there has to be a personal God.

At the risk of confusing God with what is done in God's name, Mortimer thinks that:

> On the whole, religion has had a very dangerous effect on people's moral behaviour. I believe we are capable of making better moral decisions than God has . . . and I think that is the only worthwhile moral code. That was the belief of the old 19th century atheists: that you had to behave much better because you weren't being threatened with hell-fire or the Lord of Heaven. And I think that is possible. I don't feel my behaviour is in the least bit influenced by the fear of Hell; and certainly not by that incredibly tedious immortality which my father used to compare to living forever in a great transcendental hotel with nothing to do in the evenings.

I suppose the more old-fashioned Christian would answer that eternity is something which, by our very nature, we can hardly imagine; and that the risk of damnation is not so much a threat as a fact. More progressive Christians would emphasize loving God rather than fearing Him as the proper motive for doing right. Nevertheless, the connection between morality and God (if there is one) is a key issue and some people would say it was the most important evidence for His existence. If nothing else, God must be The Good.

Humanists may attribute virtue to our natural altruism and

sympathy, and atheists to our recognition of what is sensible and useful. Clearly there are large numbers of nonbelievers every bit as virtuous as the believers. Believers can acknowledge this, admitting that most of what is morally right by their standards is also socially useful and implanted by upbringing. They do not see it as unreasonable of God to have arranged things so: after all, if God wills our welfare He will not set us standards which work ill for us in the long run. But believers feel obliged to go further. They will argue that an action is not morally right simply because it is socially desirable; the presence of an absolute demand is all-important, and the demand that gives an action its ultimate rightness is the will of the Creator. Sometimes His will is *not* recognized as useful or desirable for society. Sometimes it demands priority for an inconvenient action over a convenient one, and may even direct the self-sacrifice of the person involved. Christians recognize a number of virtues – like poverty, chastity, sacrifice, hope, submission – which are scarcely on the secular list at all but which Christians believe are on God's. The fact that they present themselves compellingly to believers as virtues seems to believers to be yet another pointer toward a source which they call God. It is a further, though less arguable, pointer that when believers seek help from that source to carry out its demands, they feel that help is given.

One meets even atheists who express anxiety at the thought of there being no religious focus for social morality to cling to, and who take leave of God with some remorse at sacrificing a useful convention. I thought I had found such a person in Marghanita Laski, when she told me she considered it would be a good thing for an atheist religion to be constructed:

Because, if people are losing their faith right, left and centre, I don't think that anarchic society without a consensus of moral code (within a very broad range) would be desirable. This is a very real loss. At the moment, working in the Arts Council, I see people leaking confidentialities all over the place, and I say that's dishonourable. But so far I haven't found a soul who thinks it matters – one or two have said they thought honour was something to do with duelling. But, no, we can't have God as a moral prop. We must be able to have a decent moral code without Gods. A great many people have – like the philosopher emperor, Marcus Aurelius. I really think the atheist virtue has to be endurance.

There is no doubt that Stoicism produced people of noble character, or that it had its influence on Christian morality, too. I have always suspected it was the true religion of the better class of English Public School. But the fact is, Stoicism appealed to a largely intellectual elite and lacked the emotional richness to satisfy as a religion. The same might be said of today's political and economic substitutes for faith. Shirley Williams, an avowedly Christian politician, remarks:

> I suppose that body for which I once worked, the Fabian Society, in its early beginnings was full of high-minded, far-sighted men and women who deeply believed that there was such a thing as a sort of humanist religion. But in the end it always fails because the attempts to build some kind of Jerusalem on earth have never worked at all; they've always fallen foul of the persistent element, I suppose, of original sin in human nature. And that's what's gone wrong, I think (to make a very sweeping judgment) with the great communist ideal. It's fallen apart at the level of its actual execution by human beings who tend to hang on to the power that they get for themselves. So I think there *has* to be a supernatural element in religion. It doesn't necessarily have to be the Christian God or, perhaps, the Christian Trinity. But that there has to be something supernatural, I think is absolutely crucial.

Humankind does not have a very good record of worshipping what it thinks are its own virtues: the roads from Nietzsche's Superman to the Third Reich, and from the Dictatorship of the Proletariat to the Gulag Archipelago have been direct and disastrous.

Religions are not constructed, they are apprehended. They were not realized by people saying 'What do we *need* and how can we give it all a religious shape?' but by people who felt something had been given to them from an independent source and who strove to find a shape in it. One reason for this shaping is to try to package the truth in forms which will preserve it and enable it to be transmitted to others. But the danger is that the packaging, preserving and transmitting get organized into vested interests. Attention to the truth itself is neglected. This is a great tragedy, because our apprehensions of the supposed God are always inadequate, the language in which we interpret them is always changing, and so are the aspects of His activity which appeal to different generations.

Dr James Hemming is a psychologist and a leading light in the British Humanist Association – a body of which Professor Ayer was president until, as he put it 'I resigned because I thought it was very sterile of them to keep on flogging a dead horse and saying "We don't believe in God – we don't believe in God!" I tried to steer it away from religion and do more to improve social conditions and so on, without saddling ourselves with aggressive disbelief. What's the good of clobbering the bishop? It's too easy!'

Dr Hemming's father was a vicar in the Church of England, and it was reading in his library that the young Hemming came to the conclusion that there were two sides to Christianity that did not fit together. On the one hand stood a wise and gentle human being, on the other all kinds of horrible statements about hell-fire and the gnashing of teeth. 'It seemed to me that somebody had messed about with the narrative.' In particular, there was the worrying tale of Jesus petulantly cursing the barren fig tree. Before long, Hemming was reading about evolution and coming to the conclusion that there was no evidence at all that man had once been perfect, had chosen to disobey God and then become fallen and incapable of redeeming himself. On the contrary, man was a slowly rising creature, even if far from perfect. Some scientists might believe that the universe was rolling downhill towards chaos, which was the theory of entropy or exhaustion of ordered energy, but human ingenuity was limitless: we might find ways of counteracting entropy. The humanist approach was to attend to things which could be improved here and now and to leave the long-term questions open. As for religion and belief in God, it was a phase in the evolution of human thought to meet people's need for explanations of what they did not understand:

> What it comes down to now, I think, is that more and more people cannot believe in an intervening God, so they are looking for an alternative; and some of them are a little strange. But this seems to me the problem of all the deistic religions: that God has been moved from the centre to the side all the time. He was thought to bring help, to control the weather and make the crops good or bad; but as human knowledge has advanced God has become less and less until he is now in just the subjective, personal area of life. Fewer and fewer people find the intervening Creator credible. On the other hand, we can't find an ultimate explanation for existence – humanists don't pretend to: they say we are living in an inscrutable situation, really. We feel that life is about the search, not about certainty, while God is an attempt to impose certainty on what is really a continuing search.

One wonders why there should be a search if there is nothing to look for. Uncertain people, says Hemming, will turn quite naturally to some source of comfort and support. But that does not have to be God. Society must come to some clear perspective on the ethical values it intends to live by: that, for example, honesty is better than dishonesty and kindness better than cruelty. And if trust goes, everything goes.

I ventured to observe that even if religious belief was in decline there was very little sign that humanism was inspiring people. Hemming responded:

> I think that is right; because the entire educational system is geared against Humanism. There has not yet been an example of the humanist state. You say that some very unpleasant things are part of human nature; but you can't expect anything else in an evolving species. Potential can be both positive and negative and human society should be so constructed as to maximise the positive and reduce the negative to a degree of harmless significance.

But did Dr Hemming really think that if only we could get the system right, earth would be fair and all men wise and good?

No, never that, because we shall always be evolving. The question is whether we are moving in a positive direction or not, and at the moment the world is stuck. It may be moving towards more information, more knowledge, but it seems to me to be profoundly stuck in terms of moving towards a richer quality of life. In order to get it unstuck you've got to get rid of the obstacles. Today we are living in an exploitive rather than a co-operative society, aren't we? You've got to have a different sort of leadership if you are going to release the dammed up potential of human capacity. There are two main sorts of leadership: the autocratic, self-aggrandising kind of people and the leader who has a natural flair for mobilising other people into effective, co-operative and purposeful action. We've had too much of the first kind and not enough of the second. All these lessons have got to be learnt and learnt fast if we are going to get humanity moving again.

I suppose it was remiss of me not to have pressed Dr Hemming as to what he meant by *positive direction*, *richer quality of life* and *get humanity moving again* – I am sure he could have explained them in terms of negative and positive potentials – but I was somewhat bemused by his enthusiasm for leadership with a natural flair for mobilizing people. I could not help feeling I had witnessed a few examples in my own lifetime and had not cared for them. Still, Dr Hemming is never a one for copping out:

The risk of belief in God and His forgiveness is that it absolves people from personal responsibility. You behave as you see fit and then you ask God's forgiveness. You play around with the natural resources of the planet, but at the back of your mind you have the idea that God will put it right in the end. Believing in God can be the abdication of human responsibility.

In other words, believers sin first, repent later. But if people really have cynically chosen such a pattern of behaviour, I cannot think of a church in the world which would endorse it, and I do not see it actually happening. I think it is one of many examples where believers are held up to ridicule for beliefs they do not hold or hold no longer. The ecological movement (since that example is conjured up) is crowded with God-fearing Christians; and it is secular science, not religion, which seeks to diminish criminal responsibility in terms of social deprivation and racial discrimination. It is not the atheists who invented the concept of sin in the first place, let alone repentance.

I find it easier to sympathize with the negative atheists, who are concerned only with the dismissal of God, than with those who still want to put something into His place. So many of the latter argue that religion is a delusion invented to meet a real human need, and then propose another delusion which barely meets half that need – the moral rather than the spiritual. When that is pointed out to them, they tend to say that people will have to grow up and pull themselves together. But this does not take seriously the fact that the believer's spiritual quest is not just for standards of right and wrong but for a sense of meaning, a sense of making sense, a sense that everything that happens to him or her is an *expression* of something and not just a brute fact. One sees this even in John Mortimer's fancy for something which would 'suffuse life with some great importance'.

It is inevitable that many who have lost, or never had, a personal feeling for the divine – and yet who retain a feeling for the right ordering of life – will try to work it out in moral terms. I suspect that this is specially true of jewish people for whom God has always been the source of social order. The Israeli philosopher of religion, Ze'ev Katz, belongs to a movement trying to propagate a humanistic Judaism; though he admits:

> The idea does appear contradictory. It was here in Jerusalem that the prophets of Israel brought the revolutionary idea of the one moral, invisible God to the Jewish people and to the world. Perhaps now, with the return of the Jewish people to this ancient land, it might also return to its ancient role as a path-finder in great human ideas. With the appearance of the critical scientific mind, the idea of linking morality, the meaning of life, the world order to the magnificent supernatural Dream Being is not acceptable any more to many people. We will have to grapple with the idea that there is man and only man with his

potentialities for good, for development, for loving his neighbour, for giving every being life before we start arguing about life after death.

Dr Katz hopes his humanistic Judaism will actually give a new lease of life to the old festivals and rituals, which he does not want to destroy because 'ritual is done in a group, and human beings need some community to belong to – not to be atomised'. He wants to preserve

> the moral standards, the tradition, the ceremonies, perhaps also the community; but without having to assert the irrational dogmas. If somebody finds in traditional religion the kind of fulfilment he needs, we believe that's just fine. What we are trying to do is to find something similar for those who cannot find it there. In other countries, if there are christians who have lost their belief, instead of just drifting in a vacuum, perhaps they should join us or follow us in some way to preserve the great ideas and traditions of Christianity, even if they have lost traditional religion.

One has only to contemplate the difference between going through the rituals of the Church in faith, and rehearsing them in disbelief (for reasons of nostalgia) to get some idea of what belief in God entails and what is lost by its absence. Why should one pray if there is nobody there to respond? Why should one adore and praise if there is nobody worthy of it? Why should one receive the sacraments if nothing is being conferred?

Asking these questions does not in itself establish that a personal God exists; but they do make the point again that it is not just morality that is being sought or even a sense of community. Nor, for christians anyway, is it a feeling of simply being in tune with the impersonal tides of the universe. I have to concede a chance that believers may be wrong, or partially wrong: they may have dressed up what *is* there in clothes that do not fit, or it may be that the clothes have no emperor. But to dismiss their faith as irrational is to miss the point. Religion does not stand on being logical, mathematical or scientific. It stands on experience and the interpretation of experience – what people *think* they experience. The fact that it is an inner experience certainly makes it difficult for the sceptic to test; but the more sane and reasonable people agree on their interpretation, and the longer that interpretation survives in its essentials, the more unreasonable it is to dismiss it as irrational. We have to take belief seriously just as we have to take unbelief seriously. The intriguing question is, how can they both be true? A logician would say they cannot, but I suspect there may be a sense in which they can.

Of all the atheists I talked to, the one I most respect is Dr Michael Goulder, one of the group of liberal theologians who in 1977 shocked the churches by publishing *The Myth of God Incarnate*. By 'myth' they did not actually mean 'fairy tale'; but four years later, after almost thirty years in the Church, Michael Goulder announced that he had lost his faith and resigned his orders. The break came hard to him. For fifteen years he had been running courses for the West Midlands clergy, passing on to them the messages of the academic theologians, so that they in turn could hand them on

> So of course it's a sad blow to them to find I've betrayed the cause. And it's a sad blow to me, too. The communion of saints has meant a lot to me. And I find it very hard to say my old bishop – Bishop Hall – who ordained me in Hong Kong, an extremely devoted and saintly man, or my old tutor, Austin Farrer, whom I respected enormously – to think that they are wrong; I don't think anybody finds it easy to leave a community where he's revered its members not only for their intellectual power but also for their sanctity.

I asked Michael Goulder why he did not feel able to join his old comrades of the *myth* group in trying to save something from the wreckage of traditional Christianity? He thought the one thing you could not do without was a belief in God, and if you took that away it was questionable what was left. His colleagues Maurice Wiles and John Hick had at least retained God, and they would say they were not 'saving something from the wreckage' but purifying the dross. Don Cupitt, on the other hand 'says he's a christian, but I can't see the sense to his saying so, because the essential elements of Christianity have vanished from his horizon'. We shall hear from Don Cupitt in person later.

I turned Dr Goulder to the claim of many Christians to know God through the Bible. He did not think that really plausible:

> You see, I think the knowledge of people through scripture depends on the faith of others from an earlier generation. Those people lived in a world where belief was indeed genuine, real and profound. But then, it was maintained by large numbers of hypotheses which we would regard as bogus. For example, people who were Jews in Jesus' time had no doubt that God had given them the Law on Mount Sinai a thousand years before. We can't accept that as a plausible basis for faith. You ask me whether the trust of one generation in another over the centuries was all nonsense – and that is a harsh word. I don't wish to be harsh about people who believed in something which was very plausible once and which has seemed plausible to me for most of my life: I am far from feeling that people are to be despised who carry on with such views. I think the difficulty is that people believe in it because they think they've experienced it; or because they think they've got some structure or proof which will hold water; or it is simply a way of looking at the world, where God seems to intervene all the time and to answer prayer.
>
> But I think the proofs don't work. I think the idea that God intervenes in our lives won't do, because there are so many times when things go wrong. And those who have testified – as so many people do – to these marvellous experiences: once you start looking at them, you find that half the people testifying are a bit cranky and it's hard to draw the line as to why certain experiences should be valid and others not.

Dr Goulder says he has never personally had a direct experience of God, and since he has left the Church has been impressed by how many serious Christians have told him the same. How is it, then, that he ever *did* believe?

Wouldn't it be nice if we were all as rational as you would like us to be? It seems to me that what we start off with is the weight of tradition on our shoulders: this is what your fathers believed – this is what your community believes. You ought not lightly to shrug all that off and hardly anybody does. I am a rather biddable person by nature, and I bought all that when I was young and, of course, I bought it with enough enthusiasm when I was prepared to be ordained.

One begins to ask questions as soon as one is preaching it and talking to people and up against the problems that are involved. What drove me out of the Church ultimately was the courses I had to teach on belief in God to responsible people including clergy. You feel rather awful after you've kept people's belief going, week after week, and then say to yourself as you go home 'I'm not sure I really believe this myself'. Gradually the penny drops, and in the end it drops with a clatter.

But does Dr Goulder never step out of his front door on a beautiful Spring day and think what a marvellous place the universe is – maybe there *is* something *out there*?

I say the first part, but not the second. It seems to me that the world *is* a marvellous place, and I'm full of wonder at it. I really enjoy nature, as indeed I enjoy a lot of things. But it always seemed to me that those religious people who say 'Don't you find the world wonderful? Well, then, you're a Christian . . .' that the 'Well, then' part is just an obvious fallacy.

It would be as hard to tell this sincere and conscientious man that he was wrong as he himself finds it to say that his saintly mentors were. Reading between his lines, however, the link that appears to have snapped between himself and his former God is that of prayer:

I don't think it ever meant a lot to me; and because of that the personal relationship with God wasn't a thing that upset me to let go. To have a structure of life in which God was important as answering prayer and so on has stopped seeming sensible to believe. So that was an incubus and I was glad to drop it.

In view of the fact that there are unbelievers – and virtuous, successful and happy unbelievers – it is fairly obvious that if God does exist belief in Him must be voluntary and not inevitable. If it is not inevitable, there can be no unchallengeable proof. There are additional reasons in Christian theology why belief should be voluntary; but as with anything that is optional, acquiring belief requires some effort of will. I do not myself think this need be the so-called 'leap of faith', believing in order to believe, though apparently that works in some cases. It seems to me that the act of will may take the simple form of a readiness to clear one's mind of clutter and open it to what may come, which I take to be the essence of prayerfulness. If there is a God, one of the charges to be levelled against Him is that apparently He allows the awareness of His existence to come to some people but not to others. But it may not be quite like that. It may be that some people can neither bring themselves to invite God in as if He existed, nor can they still their minds and leave the door open so that He can invite Himself; and there may be others again who consciously will not to entertain any such nonsense at all.

We shall return later to the intellectual case against God. The most powerful emotional case remains that of the Holocaust and of all who suffer undeservedly. Even allowing that it is, much of it, man's own fault, why does not God try harder, make His will for us plainer to spare us our agonies? I can think of no one better to take this up than a rabbi, in this case Rabbi Alan Levine of Jerusalem:

> It is like the child saying to the mother 'All you ever gave me was life. Aren't you going to give me more?' I have a distaste for people who think that everything is coming to them. We were given a world, we were given moral laws – they're very clear in Islam, in Christianity, in Judaism – but that we chose to ignore and violate them, to use them for our own power and glory, is a common profanation of God's name in God's world. What more do we want from God? Do we want God to interfere in our lives? You know,

it's a Jewish tradition that God has only the right to go so
far interfering with man. The world has been given to man
– that's clear from the Bible – and man can make the world
better or worse. The real question is, what right do we
have to ask God to interfere in our world after we've made
a mess of it? Why should God be blamed for everything
that goes on in this world? I think it's made clear in the
prophets, particularly in Amos, that justice does not work
on an individual basis. Justice works for society rather
than individuals. If society goes wrong, individuals suffer.
If society is good and healthy, then individuals flourish
and have happiness in it. Christianity is concerned with
the salvation of the individual soul, but Judaism is concerned with the salvation of society all throughout history.

Then what, I wondered, was God doing while man struggled
and fouled things up? Was He just sitting back with folded
arms, tut-tutting? Rabbi Levine sighed:

To tell you the truth, concerning this question, God has
not revealed Himself to me. It is the perennial question of
man in history. But there is a wonderful Jewish folk-song
which goes:
    The world asks an ancient question:
    La-la-la La-la-la?
    And the answer it gets back is:
    La-la-la La-la-la!

So it was all a load of rubbish, I asked? Levine responded:

I didn't say that. But the person who asks the question
knows there is no answer. And when you constantly ask a
question to which you know there is no answer, then it
becomes what you call a rubbish question – and the answer
is equally rubbish. Man has increasing knowledge about
everything in this world, but I think knowledge of God
will always elude Him.

Not an answer that would have satisfied my atheist friends.
But I went off pondering that *if* there was a God in spite of the
disasters – as Levine and a good many others accepted – then it
was a pretty drastic misuse of them to treat the disasters as

evidence for the prosecution. They were hardly good evidence for the defence of God, so perhaps they were not relevant to the case at all – in which event, where were omniscience, omnipotence and the rest? At which point, I remembered one more of Hugo Gryn's stories:

There was once a young boy in Eastern Europe who wanted to become an atheist, but nobody in the village knew how, and he needed a model. At last somebody recalled there was Jacob the Atheist living somewhere on the far side of the province. And so the boy walks for days until finally he arrives in Jacob's village and asks for him. Yes, of course – Jacob the Atheist – this is his house and his wife is in. So the boy asks, 'Is your husband Jacob the Atheist – could I see him?' 'Yes,' she says, 'but he's in the synagogue and he won't be back for a while.' Eventually, in the middle of the day, Jacob comes home. The boy says, 'I don't understand – you've been to synagogue and you're an atheist'. 'Yes, of course I am. You know they need ten people for a quorum and they needed me, so of course I went. And then I went to a circumcision – it was my great honour to hold the baby for my friend, so of course I did it. And afterwards I had to visit some sick people in the community, so I did that too.' The boy says, 'But I want to be an atheist – how do I do it?' So Jacob says to him, 'Now tell me, do you know the Bible?' The boy says, 'No, I want to be an atheist'. Jacob says, 'And do you know the Talmud – the Law?' He says, 'Of course not – I don't bother with such things'. So Jacob says finally, 'Now listen, my dear boy: what you are is an ignoramus. To be an atheist, you really have to know a lot.'

I should hate that to be thought of as just a smart put-down. After all, Jacob really was an atheist. But as Hugo Gryn remarked, after recounting his tale: 'Whenever Jews tell me they are atheists or agnostics, I always wonder whether they are well-informed people who have thought it through – or are they just ignorant?'

The enquiry must go on.

2

The Short Search

It is in the nature of religions – and perhaps even necessary – for each to claim that it alone is the true one and all the others mistaken, if not downright false. But none of them has a monopoly on the idea of God, so it seemed only fair to carry our investigation as far as the money would go. Television had its *Long Search* picturesquely conducted by Ronald Eyre from Bali to California: the best we could manage on a radio budget was a fortnight's excursion to Rome, Jerusalem, Cairo and New Delhi – our very own short search.

I actually asked Ronald Eyre whether his experience had confused or depressed him? Not a bit of it:

> I think I got clearer and merrier as a result of doing it . . .
> But one of the few occasions when I have felt like hitting
> somebody in recent years was with a BBC producer – a
> parson – who said to me, when we had done some work
> together, 'Are you really serious?' He had a really quizzic-
> al look on his face. For some people it is impossible to
> understand that one can be full of the sorts of enquiry
> which are labelled religious without belonging to one of
> the known groups.

Belonging to one of the recognized faiths is essential for most believers, nevertheless. They need its language and rituals and companionship. But the variety and conflicts of faith do not at first sight help the case in God's favour. Some emphasize outward forms, others inner experience; and among the latter some draw upon spirit possession, others upon numinous encounter with the 'wholly other', others again upon the experi-ence of total unity. There is really no coherent view of the origin of religion, except that it is some kind of response – but to what?

Is it to the natural world, the social world, the psychological world or to an actual divine world? The German romantics explored religion as a response to the world of nature. Emile Durkheim, the pioneer sociologist, interpreted it as a response to the experience of man in society. More recently it has been explained as arising from psychological states and perhaps even akin to the effects of hallucinogenic drugs. As always, one supposes, there has been the possibility that religion is the response to what actually exists 'out there' in the way of supernatural powers or spirits.

Paul Heelas, an anthropologist working at Lancaster University, reckoned that if you looked at the two or three thousand fairly distinct religions on this planet, the thing that struck you above all else was their diversity, not how much they had in common. Did not that argue (I suggested) *against* the existence of God? Heelas responded:

> Two conclusions can be drawn. One is that religions are clearly influenced by the social context in which they appear. The second is that God's message is not very clear: it must be fuzzy enough to be open to quite radically different interpretations, at the level of meaningful experience and at the level of moral and ritual response. It could be that His message has to be unclear if we are to be striving human beings. If the message was absolutely clear to everybody, we might well be inclined just to sit back in our armchairs and follow the way. If God wants us to use our faculties, then He's got to make sure that His message isn't all that clear.

The notion of a fuzzy God may sound a bit shocking, suggesting a God who is not concentrating or is playing tricks on us. But maybe it is we who have fuzzy minds, insist on injecting tribal issues that He never meant to be there.

Off we went to Italy, with the address of a hermit someone had recommended among the vineyards of Frascati, outside Rome. The setting was pure opera: a crumbling gatehouse, a rope to pull, a bell to toll, a cowled porter to open the gate and admit us to a cobbled courtyard; and from a tower overlooking it, a face like Father Christmas looked down and bellowed: 'For an Italian to be only an hour late would be a compliment – from an Englishman it is an insult!'

We made our peace, sipped an excellent malt whisky and conducted our interview. Some two hours later we found ourselves hurtling down the highway to Rome at an outrageous speed with Father Christmas – Father Farrell of the Camaldolese Benedictines, in fact – at the wheel. The gist of my challenge to him was that, having made such a commitment to the life of the spirit, he had little choice but to believe in God. Might it not all be a self-justifying word-game?

On the contrary, said the high-speed hermit, the conviction had come first, then the devotion to the life. If a monk had a crisis of faith and saw it all for a word-game, he must obey his conscience 'because God is going to judge him on that conscience and nobody else's'. It's not so easy being a hermit: we saw their larder, and it was miserable. Father Farrell, far from being the venerable seventy-year-old he looked was actually in his early fifties.

Next morning, I found myself sitting under the dome of St Peter's thinking that if God were to be found anywhere in the western world it ought to be there 'pavilioned in splendour and girded with praise'. And yet, was He there? Was God a bird to be kept in a gilded cage and sung at? Wasn't He much more likely to be outside among the pine-trees of Rome than there in that palace built more to the glory of the Popes than to the glory of God?

We went next door to the offices of the Holy Inquisition, who showed us their view but declined to be quoted on anything, and then to the more communicative Jesuits, charged by Paul VI with the task of confronting modern atheism and secularism. 'We immediately responded by setting up a special secretariat', one of them told me, 'and you don't see too much happening as a result.' He sighed at the thought of the American fundamentalists spending a billion dollars a year on airborne evangelism.

Father Jack O'Brien, a Canadian Jesuit, is in charge of electronic countermeasures against secularism. What's wrong with secularism? 'If you believe in love and justice, it's pretty hard to believe you're going to achieve them on the basis of simple human nature. Man left to himself can be pretty horrible.'

But if God's on our side, how to make sense out of human suffering?

> Pope John Paul II talks about suffering as almost being of the essence of man. When you look at the tremendous suffering in the world, you have to say it seems to be an integral part of being a human being – you just can't escape it. Of course you can't argue that it is a good thing. What you can show is that very often there comes good, where man is more compassionate for others, far more loving, more caring. On the one hand you have a constant suffering which everybody hates and tries desperately to avoid; and on the other this new moral strength and courage. It takes your breath away in amazement when you meet people who have had terrible suffering and they've come through the fire, are now almost purged, almost more human than they were before.

But if that were so, I argued, the world should become steadily more courageous, more humane . . .

> You know, good is very seldom heard from. Evil is loud and brazen, and you tend to forget all the good that is in the world, because we are so bombarded with suffering, evil and atrocities . . . But still you are caught with the basic problem, and you may want to say to the Lord that you are not going to forgive Him for all this suffering in the world. It seems to me not unchristian to put it that way, as Job did when he put the finger on God. He got a pretty dusty answer: 'Shut up – you'll never understand!' And I don't think we ever will. I think the definitive answer to belief or unbelief comes only in death. There is no way of proving belief – that would be a contradiction in terms . . . The believer understands that he is walking a tightrope all the time. He could be caught in a grand delusion, but I don't think there's any out on that. I think he has to say that belief of its very nature does not have the evidence for him to say: 'Yes, definitively that's it!' But I think you have to be able to take it and say it makes more sense to

believe than not to believe. I am not talking about grace here, or about the Lord dealing directly with you. I am talking about the evidence building up before the leap of faith. If I thought most of this evidence was ridiculous, I don't see how I could really be a believer.

So we can't explain the suffering, and we can't prove the existence of God. There is still that gap to be leapt, across which the sceptic can see nothing on the other side. But according to Father O'Brien you can pile up enough evidence to leap from. So it is still fair to ask: is it really enough?

We moved on to another Roman seat of learning – the Gregorian University – to meet an Australian, Father Gerry O'Collins. As we sat talking, the lights failed, as they do frequently in that part of Rome, and it gave us a pretty picture of two men talking about God in the dark. Nothing daunted, Father O'Collins took up Jonathan Miller's complaint about the cruelty that God permits His children to inflict upon one another:

I agree that there are mysterious sufferings that are not caused by human beings. But really, in our world today, eighty to ninety per cent of our pain and suffering is caused by other human beings. We are cruel to one another, we waste money on massive and terrible weapons, we let children starve, we could wipe out leprosy if we wanted to, but we don't.

GP: But why have leprosy in the first place? That seems pretty unreasonable.

O'C: Well, yes, that's true. That's part of the ten per cent. It's surely a challenge to human beings to get rid of these things scientifically. God's given us the freedom to do it. We could have done it decades back if we'd put our mind to it. I do agree that there is a mysterious residue of suffering that we human beings cannot do something about, but there's a tremendous amount we can do. In short, before putting God on trial, I would rather put human beings on trial for their cruelty and incompetence. When we've fixed that up we can think about charging God with what's left.

Skilfully played, I thought. But if God was the Creator, why did He make creatures that got themselves into these appalling situations. Surely He could have contrived something better?

Well, He could have taken our freedom away from us, or offered us such instant and enormous rewards for using it properly that He would be treating us like children.

GP: Happy children . . .

O'C: Happy children, but certainly not mature adults. And I don't think it's worthy of God to create beings with freedom and then turn round and take it away – bribe us all the time into doing the right thing.

I suggested that a few well-placed miracles could tidy up a lot of our doubts and fears. Nothing excessive – just a few signs in the skies, some tremendous healings, an earthquake reversed . . . Said O'Collins:

The philosopher David Hume gave the answer to that a couple of centuries ago, when he said that even if someone came back from the dead and lived on earth again and was seen by millions, he still would not believe – because, according to Hume, God simply doesn't work miracles and no amount of evidence would ever convince him. Even if we had films of the Resurrection or tape recordings of the Risen Lord speaking to His disciples, people would always say they were faked, or interpret them in another way. I think our God has given us enough light, enough reasons for believing, but He doesn't want to hit us over the head and force us into belief. Our freedom, our willingness to see what the message is, is being respected.

Now this argument from free will seems to me absolutely crucial to the justification of God – if there is a God. It does not, as Gerry O'Collins like Frances Young indicated, explain away all our suffering, let alone the worst examples. But it helps. It forces us – as a race – to acknowledge that we could have avoided much of our suffering and could eliminate still more if we put our minds to it. Christian believers, however, mindful of original sin, cannot be too optimistic about the chances of achieving paradise on earth: and at this point, some unbelievers will jump in crying: 'Exactly! For this supposed free will is an illusion. We are programmed, we are determined, everything we do is just another event in a chain of causes and effects which began long before our individual selves came on the scene. Insofar as we have the illusion of freedom, it extends only to the merest trivialities.'

This, too, I think, has to be taken very seriously. Even if we do have free will it cannot be total. Clearly we have to take a huge bundle of characteristics and situations as given. Free will (if it exists) entails choosing from given alternatives, and the choice is often limited or biassed. But why should we be conscious of a choice – morally conscious that we might have made a better choice – if there isn't one really? And what chooses if not our will, our *ability* to act on the basis of accepting this and rejecting that? The fact is, we act *as if* we had free will so persistently that it seems to me to merit the description of free will – even to the point of being able to deny it. In fact it is rather similar to belief in God: one may not be able to prove it one hundred per cent, but there is enough for many people to approach life *as if* there were a God and to call that believing in Him. Even though it still leaves room for others, reasonably, not to believe.

We left Rome for Jerusalem in Israel-Palestine-Jordan – everybody's Holy Land. Rabbi Gryn had warned us:

> The fact is that in Israel today there is an unexpected amount of agnosticism; but actually, what you find there is secularism. In my language, it's idolatrous. Idolatry is nothing but the substitution of the material for the spiritual. It's a very attractive doctrine and Jews happen to be particularly prone to it. When you read the Hebrew Bible, it's full of warnings against idolatry; and they wouldn't be doing all that warning if it wasn't a real problem. So we understand this phenomenon and we haven't overcome it yet.

Morale was low in Israel. Inflation was running at the rate of four hundred per cent a year. The Lebanese operation was a mess. The stranglehold of the religious parties upon politics was vexatious, and the outbreaks of religious terrorism against the

Arabs shameful. But at least in democratic Israel one can say and discuss these things openly; as can Uri Avneri, Tel Aviv magazine editor and scourge of the Israeli political and religious establishment. Uri, when I met him, was incensed at the way the observances of the Orthodox Jewish minority were being imposed upon the majority either by blackmail or by secular law:

> Israel was created by people who did not believe in God. Half the pioneers who built the country were hard-core atheists. They came from Russia and Poland with socialist utopian ideas and they totally rejected Jewish religion because it was identified in their eyes with the exile culture which they hated and against which they were rebell-ing . . .
> My generation which was brought up in Jewish schools in what was then called Palestine in the 1930s had a great contempt for the Jewish culture in Europe. We had what you could almost call an anti-semitic education. When we heard about the holocaust, there was a reaction – a great wave of repentance and regret. And when the State came about, Ben Gurion, our leader (who was a total atheist) had to compromise with the religious people both inside the country and outside . . .
> I think Israel would be healthier and happier today if it were an atheistic state. Religion provides the dynamic power for all the nationalistic, chauvinistic and even neo-fascistic movements you have in Israel today, working for annexation and even the expulsion of the Arab popula-tion . . . You could say that in this country there are a lot of people who don't believe in God but do believe that God promised us this country and told us to expel or kill the inhabitants. There's a fight against laws of religious coer-cion imposed on Israel by the secular parliament of a secular state, and against an extreme kind of racialism mixed with religious fundamentalism.

Uri Avneri's language will sound like treason to many sup-porters of Israel both at home and abroad. But I was more concerned with his theology – or antitheology – than with his politics. Was the State of Israel conceivable without its religion? Uri answered:

> I feel in myself certain moral concepts which I believe are Jewish. I believe this new religion being evolved today is a reactionary throwback that puts Judaism back three thousand years. I would like to see Judaism grow up by becoming humanistic. This was the spirit of the founders of modern Zionism. The Jews have been held together by their religion throughout the ages. In this sense it had a function. It was a kind of substitute for the state. But now that we are becoming a normal nation based on territory, we don't need religion any more.

Even so, in deploring the rise of religious fundamentalism in Israel, Islam, even the United States, Uri Avneri felt obliged to blame it on the *failure* of western liberal humanist attitudes. And this was underlined by Professor Werblowski, a Jerusalem specialist in comparative religion. Twenty years ago, he would have prophesied a relentless trend towards atheism in Israel as in other societies:

> But the orthodox, or the believers, seem to have lost the sense of insecurity which they had a few decades ago. Then they felt they were an embattled minority trying to hold their own against the aggressive secularism of the modern age, decked out with all the symbols of modern science and progressive ethics. Now I think the boot's on the other leg. The secularists are on the defensive. They realise that secularism has not produced a better world. Fifty years ago you could say all kinds of nasty things about mediaeval fanaticism and the Inquisition and wars of religion. Well, they (the secularists) fought worse wars, and not in the name of God. So people generally feel they've been left in the lurch. Not only Communism is the God that failed, but secularism as a whole. More specifically as to Israel: the pioneering spirit that turned the waste land into the Garden of Eden may have provided enough spiritual nourishment for the first generation; but the second and third generations are gradually discovering the emptiness behind it. Maybe because they no longer

have the same challenges to tackle, they feel perhaps there is something in that old tradition which our ancestors managed to keep alive, in spite of the pogroms and suffering and humiliation, that we should go back to.

I asked one Christian scholar living in Israel what most impressed him about Judaism as he saw it around him. 'I think it is faithfulness,' he said, 'faithfulness to the Law. The best of them don't go whoring after strange gods. They work at the Law, they live the Law and they are content with the fruit that comes from working at it. That faithfulness is tremendously impressive. It can take them through the most dreadful circumstances; and I think it's a reflection of the faithfulness of God.'

Surely there must have been amazing faithfulness on both sides for many – or any – Jews to have stayed loyal to their particular vision of God despite all tribulations. Nevertheless the fact that, as Alan Levine had put it, 'Judaism is concerned with the salvation of society' clearly makes it vulnerable to drastic changes in society brought about by secular means.

But perhaps, if we are looking for God in Israel, we should see the modern story of the Jews as a parable for all mankind. That is how it appeared to a man called Bernard, a survivor of Auschwitz, whom I met near Bethlehem:

So we are all in the gas chamber now . . . The old power games are still going on, and we think we are playing with rifles and shot-guns. There's an insanity happening, and we're ready to blow away the whole planet for our right-eousness, a point of view, an interest, and we call that God on Our Side. Now the whole world is a potential gas chamber, and the question is, who's going to be the Nazi? Last night, looking out on Bethlehem – beautiful lights, the moon, a bright star there – I said, 'My God, this is the area in which monotheism originated, and look at the conflict going on here right now.' And if we can re-examine what this idea of God is, without all the details of how, but get down to the essence, we're all of us saying: 'We believe in God'. So let us examine what that means. What would be the behaviour of a person who is trying to imitate God? And to me, if it includes anything of ideology for political purposes, or power and control – then it's not God. We're talking about something else.

And that lies at the heart of the atheist critique: that so much religion is not about anything that deserves to be called God. It is about something else.

I sat on the Mount of Olives just above Gethsemane, looking across at the soldierly walls of the Old City. 'Jerusalem the golden, with grinding traffic cursed – Upon your battered ruins three faiths have wreaked their worst . . .' The original actors would hardly recognize a stone of it today. The Jerusalem of Jesus was knocked down, ploughed up and buried nineteen hundred years ago; the Temple of Solomon long before that; and the holy city of Mohammed (towards which the faithful prostrated themselves until orders were changed to Mecca) in its turn. Yet all three faiths, Christian, Jewish and Muslim, kept coming back to the ruins and raking them over, as if God had been buried here and we could dig Him up again. But if you are prepared to be broad-minded about it, the gods have even older cemeteries – in Egypt. The pyramids were the tombs of men who claimed to be gods, and never more so than when they were dead. What might they have to tell us?

We flew on to Cairo, or rather to the ruins of Memphis, where I happen to know an articulate young archaeologist called Michael Jones, who is excavating something to do with the cult of Apis, the sacred bull. He and his team live in a bleak concrete box near the site, and from the flat roof the horizon is jagged with pyramids. That is the tantalizing thing about the religion of ancient Egypt: its relics are so well preserved and yet so mysterious – so near and yet so far. As Michael Jones explained, we can turn the inscriptions into something that makes sense, but we cannot be sure it is the sense the ancient Egyptians gave to it:

We don't really understand the way in which the ancient Egyptians spoke about their gods. The different words they used to describe the attributes of various gods can be loosely translated into modern English words for which we understand the meaning. But to extend the meaning back into ancient Egyptian thought, I would think, is impossible. We're talking about a period of man's history which spanned nearly three thousand years. Even within that period, ideas must have changed radically. And one of the problems is the lack of records at certain times and the enormous wealth of them at others, which immediately puts a bias on one's knowledge.

Nevertheless from certain communities you could get a picture of the common people enjoying a close relationship with their local gods, celebrating their festivals and, with the help of a trained priesthood, going through the proper ceremonials so that the right things would happen at the right time. Jones does not think you can talk about Monotheism in ancient Egypt, though a particular person might talk about *his* personal god, to whom he made offerings and whom he might even take abroad with him on a trip.

And weren't the pharaohs gods, I asked?

The king was never described in Egyptian literature as a fully fledged god in the same terms as the great gods of the Egyptian pantheon. But he was certainly divine. There was no idea of him becoming divine at death after living a human life, nor of his becoming divine by virtue of his coronation. It seems he was a divine being from his conception.

Jones went on to recount the myth of the god Osiris, murdered, dismembered and then reassembled posthumously to beget his son Horus. The deceased king of Egypt was always regarded as Osiris and his successor as Horus, an intriguing forerunner of crucifixion, resurrection, incarnation; though I think, myself, we can be too easily seduced by such resemblances; by, for example, the tendency of Egyptian gods to come in threes which, nevertheless, retain their separate identities and do not amount to the Christian Trinity. Michael Jones went on:

The ancient Egyptians did not think in abstracts, which is what we, with our legacy from the classical world, do. We put things into categories and we think in terms of theology, politics, philosophy. There are no words for these in ancient Egyptian, and although they had hundreds of gods, yet they had no word for religion. For them every single thing was part of a great unity in diversity, and the unity was seen in some cases as present in the king . . .

It seems to me that what we read in the ancient Egyptian religious literature are explanations and descriptions for things we observe today and for which we use science and psychology. The ancient Egyptians used another form of jargon, if you like. They explained natural forces, natural events, the cycle of life and death, night and day – they explained these things in terms of the powers within them that made things work. And central to ancient Egyptian thinking was a concept which they called *maaht*, for which we have no English translation. It means something like order, it means something like truth, it means something which is a balance between what we call good and evil, between light and dark. It means the balance which maintains a system and an order. And the reason why ancient Egyptian culture continued in the form it did for so long is that in ancient Egyptian minds, the person of the king and queen and the gods and goddesses they represented were bound up with the very earth itself. The land was within the king, and if the king died or fell ill, then there was danger in the land.

GP: But surely we know better?

Jones: We think we do. I don't think we do. My opinion is that we are just different. Within ancient Egyptian society this belief functioned very well. The Egyptians maintained that order – that *maaht* – against enormous odds, and it lasted three thousand years. Not that they denied foreign deities. The ancient Egyptians didn't regard foreign religions as evil in the same way that the monotheistic religions of today cut out foreign religions.

'Well, there!' the atheist can say, 'the perfect example of the God-fiction being used to underpin the ordering of society and the pre-scientific search for explanations!' And to his embarrassment, the atheist may find himself supported by the Christian fundamentalist. But the liberal Christian believer will not be discouraged. For a start, he will be rather envious of a way of thinking that managed to unify nature, society and worship. He no longer believes that these manipulate each other magically, but he can still see in the ancient Egyptian system a devoted attempt to make sense of the divine will and to live in harmony with it. Today's believer has the very same objectives.

This applies to modern Egypt's main religion, Islam, which stems from the same semitic roots as Judaism and Christianity. Islam is far less monolithic than many westerners believe – it has its catholics and protestants, its mystics, fundamentalists and heretic fringes, just like Christianity – but in general what impresses about it is its simplicity and the intense concentration of its worship. While we were in Rome a Catholic student of Islam, Father Tom Michel, told us:

> I've trooped into a mosque sometimes with thirty people while prayers were going on, and not a soul would turn their head. It's to be given a concentration and respect which I find really impressive. And another thing I find impressive is the way prayers are not supposed to take you out of your daily existence. You see people praying at the back of their shops, and construction workers at noontime will lay down a newspaper on the street and pray on the paper. It's a way of rededicating yourself to God five times over during the day. Our monks do it during their office – but they are the very few among Christians.

Father Michel warned us that we would not find atheism or agnosticism in the world of Islam to anything like the extent we found it among Christians and Jews. He thought it had something to do with Muslims seeing themselves as a Third Force against western materialism and atheistic communism – in other words, as a racial and political badge of identity. Gai Eaton, an English Muslim, told us:

> For the Muslim doubt – as, I suppose, for the Christian a few centuries ago – is very much a whispering of Satan. If it does arise, you reject it rather as a chaste man – if he has a passing fancy for a pretty girl in the street – dismisses the thought as being quite irrelevant to his life. He doesn't dignify it with his attention. As for the Jewish notion of

protesting, arguing, accusing God – not only is it un-
acceptable, it's unthinkable. The western-educated Muslim knows what you're talking about; but to the traditional, ordinary Muslim, this is a crazy question. The sun may
kill a man who is out in the desert and doesn't have enough
water; but you don't look up at the sun and say: 'You
wicked sun, you killed this man!'

GP: But does God intervene in human affairs?

Eaton: All the time, to such an extent that Islam is not
interested in miracles. It isn't that there are no miracles,
but they have nothing to do with proving the power of
God. Every single moment of time is in His hands, and if
He chooses at any particular moment to disregard the laws
He has made for Himself, then clearly there is nothing in
the least strange about it.

It seemed even clearer that we were not going to have much
luck with finding atheists in Cairo or even discovering the
Muslim equivalent of our Jewish and Christian progressives.
We had hopes when we were introduced to Abdullah Schleifer,
an American Jewish convert to Islam, a refugee from drugs and
the Beat Generation, but he rapidly disabused us:

I am suggesting that I, as a Muslim, am closer to a
traditional Christian than a modern Christian is. And I
think I am closer to a traditional Jew than a modern Jew –
reformed or conservative or any of the new modern varia-
tions. In Islam we've never had the grace of either a
reformation or a renaissance. The critics say: 'Why is it
you Muslims haven't had your reformation or renaissance
yet?' I say – thanks be to Allah! Why is it the mosques are
full and hundreds of millions of people are still trying to
live out their lives in accordance with their religion? It's
because we haven't had a renaissance or a reformation. If
you ask me to come back and see you tomorrow I shall say
'Inshallah! – If God wills!' Christians said it once – Jews,
too. But they don't any more.

As delicately as I could, I asked Abdullah Schleifer if a
traditional Muslim would be shocked at the idea of putting God
on trial?

Oh, thoroughly! I mean, I'm shocked. The whole notion is so outrageous – it seems to suggest such a rebellious spirit and such a lack of gratitude. The very notion is by definition a negation of Islam, for Islam is the peace that comes to you by grace of your utter submission to the will of God. So the notion that I put God on trial is so outrageous that the traditional Muslim would say: 'That's my definition of unbelief'.

So God – Allah – was running the show and there was no room for complaints. Islam made Christian fundamentalism seem positively flexible. There was no room, either, for anyone but Allah; as Mohammed Sherif El-Herrawi, an Egyptian businessman, told us with great emphasis:

No! In Islam there is no intermediate between man and God. God is there! God is with us now! There's only One God, so powerful, so strong, so merciful. But He punishes! Because if He is merciful all the time it would be chaos . . . We have no saints here! God is there! God is here! God is inside!

And I got less than nowhere when I tried to interest Dr Zahira Abdin – who is a kind of Muslim Mother Teresa – in the idea that there might be a feminine aspect of Allah:

Allah has to be much more purified than everything. While we are told that your mind can lead you to belief in this great creative mind, it cannot lead you to have a complete picture of the nature of this Allah. We can know so much of His qualities, but He is unlike anything, He is above anything, He is over anything feminine. Why should He need feminine? He is not a man who needs a woman just to be with her. He does not need a companion or a son to help Him in this or that. Otherwise He is not – He is not the all-powerful, all-knowing, all-able God!

After these blows at the communion of saints, Christian feminism and the doctrine of the Trinity, Chris Rees and I packed hastily and left for Delhi. Christianity, as I understand it, is not trying to equip God with a girl-friend and a troupe of helpers, but it was plainly futile to try to convince Muslims that there could be any development of their very clear-cut monotheism that was not a blasphemy. And, come to that, I know Jews who feel much the same. If there is a God, there is remarkably little agreement how He operates.

India is one of my old stamping-grounds as a foreign correspondent and I love it dearly. What is more, I deeply respect its people for the way they tolerate the intolerable and make sense of lives that often seem cruelly senseless, largely thanks to a religion – Hinduism – which may appear superficially primitive to the newcomer but is actually highly developed. It has its nasty corners, but it works, and it does so through a mythology which leaves Christians as outraged as Muslims (though it manages to accommodate the Sikhs, Buddhists and Jains without much difficulty). There are even many in the west who regard India as a specially holy country with a hotline to God that others have not got.

I put that to an old friend of mine, P. C. Chatterji, a philosopher who was once Director General of All India Radio. He put his cards on the table:

> I'm an atheist, though I respond deeply to mystical verse. Hopkins appealed to me very much, Francis Thompson and people like that . . . I'm afraid the trouble in India is that we are concerned about that hotline, but not with who may be at the other end of it. We are bothered about the paraphernalia of religion, but we have forgotten the real substance. I wish I could call it the pursuit of God. But it is the pursuit of ritual and the outward signs minus the inward spiritual graces. The very big problem today is the clash between these manifestations of religion as observed by one group and another – I think we really need to curb them. An important thing in India has been the question of freedom of religion: but what has tended to happen is that there has been not only freedom but licence so far as pomp and show is concerned. This business of taking out processions: they've got no sanction in scripture, new traditions are being built up every day of taking out these processions, and they are just a show of strength. If religious observance is not some sort of communication with the divinity, what is its real significance?

Chatterji ('Tiny' to his friends) thinks there are very few atheists in India, even among the intellectuals. Logically, he thinks, most Indian religion can be reduced to predestination, although everyone works hard enough to get the good things of life and only resorts to fatalism when they are disappointed. How do Indians cope with the problem of suffering, then?

On the one hand there is the doctrine of Karma – there is this cycle of lives, and you undergo suffering in this one because you committed sins in a previous life. It's a sort of punishment for sins which unhappily you don't even remember. The other way of looking at suffering is to say that – like the whole world – it is in a sense illusory. It appears as suffering to you because you cannot see reality as a whole. If you had this knowledge, you would not see it as suffering. . .

As a philosopher I must say the whole idea of worshipping God is self-contradictory. I mean, if things are predestined, there's nothing you can do to change them. God could only change for the worse, and being perfect He can't do such a ridiculous thing. I think that when people go to pray, they are trying to come to terms with reality. . .

As an atheist I am not at all depressed at the prospect of there being no afterlife. I have lived long enough – I'm sixty-three – and I certainly wouldn't want to live again. This idea of Heaven is a bit of insanity – just fancy living in a state of perfection! You can't love, because who will want it? I don't want Heaven, I want to be finished soon.

I only hope that, if there is a Heaven, I shall meet the civilized Tiny Chatterji in it – not too soon – if only to see his pleasure at it. But we left our Indian Stoic and went off to see a social scientist called Ashish Nandi who works in a dilapidated imperial bungalow among the old Civil Lines of Delhi. Although an up-to-date westernized agnostic, Dr Nandi attaches great importance to the survival of religion in India because he thinks the average Hindu peasant needs the language of religion to handle his social and political choices:

I particularly want to emphasise the fact that in India a very large number of the people use religious idiom to express their sufferings, their understanding of man-made sufferings, their understanding of oppression, their understanding of the human predicament, and to conceptualise it. I personally feel there is a need today to restore some of these categories within the public discourse.

But this sounded dangerously like the communalized politics, the provocative parading and slogan-shouting which Chatterji had been denouncing. Dr Nandi protested that he was far from advocating a Hindu State, though Hindu originally meant everyone living in Hind, in India. Hinduism was not a religion in the Christian sense: it was really a way of life and it had had profound effects on Indian forms of Christianity and Islam. Dr Nandi declined to accept the argument that Hinduism, with its plethora of gods and goddesses, was in any sense more primitive than the monotheistic religions: 'Monotheism does not necessarily mean religious development or advancement. Some forms of Christianity have a touch of pantheism about them. For example, in Mexican Catholicism many of the saints look like some of the Aztec gods.'

Chris Rees and I had hoped to meet a genuine Indian guru in his native habitat and had got wind of one – Pilot Baba, an ex-Indian Air Force ace – who operated from Agra and specialized in getting buried alive. Unfortunately, when we got there, Pilot Baba had gone underground. Dr Nandi did not think we had missed very much: gurus like that were only popular in urban areas, and he deplored the way they felt it necessary nowadays to claim their teaching was compatible with quantum physics and cosmology: 'Any religion which has to justify itself in terms of the latest theories of modern science has admitted defeat.' But why was the doctor, although not himself a believer, so protective towards religion?

Because, like many people of my kind, I fear this juggernaut called secular scientific value. I think it is universalising the entire world. We have not only produced, for the first time, a universal drink like Coca Cola, universal dress like blue jeans, universal music like pop: we are producing a generation that thinks the same way, eats the same way, dances the same way and has no problem communicating across cultures and countries. People like me see religion as a possible barricade against the encroachment of this universalising, homogenising value. I don't think India needs more religion. What India needs to do is to protect its various religious traditions as a source of cultural plurality. I think one of the saddest parts of the Indian development effort has been that it has tended to homogenise society. . .

So what we had here, it seemed, was a social engineer who saw belief as healthy, but not necessarily true. That, said Dr Nandi, was a typically modern response. Modern science had forced a split between beauty and truth:

Previously, if something was true, it was also beautiful and it was also good for you. Now we have this trichotomy: the scientist is concerned with truth, the humanities with beauty and social engineering with human well-being. Something which is good for you may not be true, something which is good may not be beautiful, something which is beautiful may not be true. This trichotomy I do not think is settled. As for the existence of God, it is part of a language. You can neither prove nor disprove it.

India was proving alarmingly unspiritual, so I went and sat for a while in the famous Birla Temple in New Delhi, surrounded by images of gods and goddesses, of monkeys, elephants and bulls, as the worshippers around me – men and women of the twentieth century – practised what appeared to be superstitious paganism at its most primitive. But was it? If there were a God, the creator of all, could He have allowed those people to follow complete lies for centuries, and reserved the truth only for Christians, Jews and Muslims? Despite the differences, one had only to read the inscriptions on the temple walls to see how universal they were: 'God is One. He is omnipresent, omnipotent, omniscient and the creator of the whole universe. God is within and without all beings, both near at hand and far away.' It might not take one very far in the dimension of intellectual progress, but it took one very deep.

Pilot Baba might be incommunicado, but we had the opportunity to go even higher towards the top. The Dalai Lama –

popularly described as the God King of Tibet – normally lives in exile up in the foothills of the Himalayas, a trip we were nervous of making because of the rioting that was going on in the Punjab. Fortunately His Holiness was visiting New Delhi, enjoying the lush comforts of a large suite in the Ashoka Hotel. Having met him some thirty years earlier, I knew that the correct ceremonial was to exchange white silk scarves with him. He travels with a bale of them for the purpose, but how was *I* going to get hold of one to give him? I settled for a bunch of flowers and thrust them into his embarrassed hands the moment he entered the room – rather spoiling the prayerful gesture he was trying to aim at me. I did not get my scarf until the end of the interview, when Chris got one too.

The Dalai Lama was enthroned when he was only five and is now barely fifty years old. He is sturdily built, though stooping, crewcut, bespectacled, robed in maroon and orange, with purple socks and a stout pair of brogues on his feet. Most Tibetans are jovial by nature, and the Dalai Lama chortles and smiles a good deal, especially when asked questions he has no intention of answering. He speaks English quite well, uttering it in swift groups of words with what a westerner would probably describe as a Chinese accent.

Devout Tibetans believe the present incumbent to be the 14th incarnation of the 15th century Tibetan Buddhist abbot Dge-'dun-grub-pa, a man of such holiness that he was qualified to escape the endless cycle of rebirth but who, out of his compassion for mankind, chose to be born again and again in order to be of service. Thus the Lama I met was not so much a god as a recycled saint. Was sanctity what I experienced? Not exactly, but there was certainly an unpretentious spirituality about him. He is also very keen on collecting evidence of reincarnation, and regrets having forgotten his own previous existence; though his mother told him there was a time, in his childhood, when he could remember it.

I could not resist asking him if it was true, as some people said, that he *was* a god?

Certainly not. Now this much depends on the interpretation of the word God. 'God King' (*he laughed*) – it's

difficult to say. You see, I always regarded myself as a
humble Buddhist monk.

But did he believe in a God who created the world and who
loved and cared for everyone? The Dalai Lama went into a long
dissertation about suffering being the result of wrong actions
motived by mental defilements like anger, desire and attach-
ment. Both suffering and the permanent happiness known as
Nirvana or enlightenment came from one's own action: 'Nobody creates these things except one's own action. Now action
comes from mental consciousness. So, to summarize, the
creator is something like one's own consciousness.' The important thing was to find an experienced teacher, first the Buddha
himself and then some monk or group of monks to be one's
companion:

> As far as Buddhism is concerned, the learning is very
> important. Without learning, it is very difficult to prac-
> tise, and without practice you cannot get the real experi-
> ence. So, you see, learning and meditation should go
> together. . .
> We believe there are limitless Buddhas. So all these
> Buddhas – in a certain way, like God – are all-powerful,
> all-knowing, all-merciful: except all these come through
> training, training, training. You can get their advice and
> blessing.

But how was it, I asked, that Buddhism had become so
insignificant in India, the land of its birth? For three reasons,
said the Dalai Lama. First, the kings and princes who had been
supporting it lost interest. Second, the Buddhist philosophers
had been defeated in argument with the Hindus. And third, the
Buddhist monks had not behaved well and had gone in for
strange forms of yoga involving sex, blood and corruption.
Gradually people had lost respect for them.

The Dalai Lama insisted that provided you were properly
trained to concentrate the mind in meditation you could get all
the spiritual experience you needed 'with this life, with this
body'. He had friends who had spent many years in the
mountains, where they had the chance to concentrate all their

energies, and they had the power to leave their physical bodies, go where they liked and return again. Could he do that himself? Unfortunately, no.

The Dalai Lama travels and teaches abroad a great deal and takes a kindly view of other religions, provided people find them of practical value. 'But if their way of life is something different, and religion becomes a special thing in church or cathedral, then it is not much use.'

I kept trying to nudge the Lama towards saying whether or not he believed in a supernatural God – and he knew it. He kept responding with Tibetan grins and chuckles, until eventually I cornered him and extracted the following:

The pureness of ultimate consciousness is there as a basis or seat and for that we can develop anything. But if one accepts it as a God then, no. Certainly you get some mysterious experience due to certain other forces. Then if you call God – all right. Now you see I always believe each different religion. If we use the Sanscrit word *dharma* that maybe has a wider meaning. Some scholars stick to religion as meaning a sort of fate based on God. Then Buddhism is not that kind of religion. Some people say Buddhism is the signs of mind – a philosophy, perhaps.

Also some people say Buddhism is a kind of atheism. In any case, each different *dharma* has a special quality and you have to choose one suitable to your own mental disposition. For certain people the Christian faith is much more effective than Buddhism, for certain people Buddhism is much more effective than Christianity – that I believe. Despite the fundamental differences, all are serving and helping humanity in order to develop their own heart. Now that is what we need today. Today our science and technologies have reached a state our forefathers never even dreamed of. Yet we remain under terror and anxiety. Why, with more facilities and material development, does the human being remain all tension and suspicion? This shows definitely that we are lacking something that I believe is the warmth of a good heart. I think we need a genuine sense of brotherhood and sisterhood on the basis of compassion and love.

Unexceptionable; but how? I suggested a Christian would say brother- and sisterhood under the Fatherhood of God. 'Yes, all right!' said the Dalai Lama cheerfully. 'People who believe in God the Father can really take brothers and sisters!'

It seemed to me that we had been listening to a generous and sophisticated form of humanism – though humanism with some important differences. There was, for example, little inclination to admire the human potential for worldly achievement. There was a good deal of systematic Stoicism, and there was the obsession with the cycle of rebirth and how to escape it. I knew from experience that the average Buddhist peasant of Southeast Asia practised a variety of the faith that was much less dependent upon mental techniques and much more concerned with images, stories and the possibility of supernatural intervention than what I had been hearing. Nevertheless, if anyone wanted a highly moral, god-free religion which seemed proof against the worst dangers of do-it-yourself humanism – somebody with a great deal of time to spare for meditation and study – they might do worse than follow the Dalai Lama. I should find it too systematic, too unstimulating, too self-centred and culturally too remote for myself; but it is hard to quarrel with its gentleness and tolerance, which is more than one can say for many other faiths.

Chris Rees and I shopped hastily for souvenirs in the New Delhi handicrafts emporium and staggered back to London with our tape recordings. We had been pretending to each other that we were on a mission to find God in three continents, but in truth we had never expected to do so, and we had not – and we had. We had found many other people's ideas of God, or His absence, but the outstanding impression was precisely of that fuzziness Paul Heelas had described and which was so suspicious. From the Catholics one might have gathered that God was shouting but Man was deaf; from the Jews that Man was shouting but God was deaf; from the Muslims, that there was no question of argument at all; and from the Dalai Lama, that there was nobody to argue with. Throughout the journey we had kept meeting people – believers, agnostics and downright atheists – who emphasised the importance of behaving, in one way or another, *as if* there were a God. They felt it was useful, they felt it was healthy, they felt it somehow worked. Why should that be so if there was no God? As to what people meant by God anyway (which might seem to be the key question) there were as many answers as witnesses.

Readers will have detected already that I am not one of those who has been given the answers in one dramatic revelation at a particular place and a particular time. Nevertheless, my producer would keep trying, putting me down under the dome of St Peter's or in the courtyard of the Birla Temple and switching on the recording machine to see what happened to me: I have transcribed some of my impressions above. When we got back to England, he had one last try.

And so I came to Glastonbury; to holy Glastonbury with its mystical earth-forces, its magic spring, its miraculous thorn-tree, its rumours of Arthur and Avalon and Joseph of Arimathaea, 'and did those feet in ancient time walk upon Glastonbury Tor?' Well, I doubt it. Glastonbury is a very pretty place indeed. But more and more I became convinced that places are made holy by the holiness of the people who have lived and prayed there, and with apologies to St Dunstan – who really was there – I don't think Glastonbury has got it. For me, there were no holy vibrations and no more presence of God than on Hampstead Heath. If places could not put me in touch with God, we had better go and meet some of the people who claimed to know Him personally.

3

Is There Anybody There?

The Ecumenical Institute at Tantur, just outside Bethlehem, is a tasteful but strangely lifeless place. It is full of worthy ecumenical people doing worthy ecumenical things; but if I were a militant atheist I should come away from a visit there gleefully satisfied that nothing was brewing in it which was likely to make more people convinced of the reality of God. Its most explosive occupant – Bernard, the concentration camp survivor – was something of an embarrassment to the place. But then, perhaps there are enough explosives in the Holy Land already.

Tantur tries to avoid odious comparisons in the world of faith, and it saddens Donald Nicolls, the director, that he has never yet heard a profession of faith from one of his distinguished visiting speakers which did not somehow denigrate other faiths by comparison. The thread he looks for in approaching other world religions is the thread of holiness:

> It seems to me you have holy people in all the religions which I know, and therefore I take all those seriously . . . They say that a holy person creates a space around him or her in which it is easier for other people to be good; and I think that's true. And it's true also, I think, of the relationship of holy people to the animal creation. It's a constant throughout the world's religions that when people become holy, the animals and the birds and the fishes feel at home in their presence.
>
> I don't see that there's any other way that the world religions can come together except by each of them deepening their pursuit into the depths of their own being. And then they meet in the depths. Of course there are doctrinal questions which arise out of this, but the doc-

trinal questions are a sort of secondary symptom . . . I think this is what the saints in all the world's religions are saying to us. You may know the Zen saying: 'I pointed to the moon, and a fool looked at my finger.' The experts spend all the time examining your finger and saying: 'Well, it is *so* long', instead of looking where the finger is pointing. Doctrine is only important as an expression of the reality, it must not be taken as the reality itself.

With which I agreed: it was one of my conclusions from *Priestland's Progress*. But I was looking now for ways of knowing this supposed God. Perhaps the holy knew the trick, but with faith apparently losing its grip over so much of the western world, wasn't it about time God did something to convince the rest of us that He existed and ought to be taken seriously? Nicolls replied with a variant of what I had heard from O'Collins in Rome and Levine in Jerusalem:

You know, one of the things that strikes me about Africans, as opposed to us, is that we find life difficult to take except on our own terms. For Africans, life on any terms is good. We've got into the habit of thinking: 'I'm only going to accept life *if* I've got a good education, a good job, I'm sure of a pension and I'm going to be healthy.' Well, you know, that isn't life. I read these demographers who say that the number of children we're having is going down – that our population is losing its taste for life.

I was coming to accept this argument, that it was not really reasonable (if there was a God) to expect Him to hand us our life skinned and filleted on a plate, with vegetables cooked to perfection, *à la carte*. But surely there must be some direct experience of God's intervention in our life for it to be reasonable for us to believe in Him at all? Had Donald Nicolls any such experience himself? There was a long silence – and a sigh:

You put me in a difficult situation here. Because the answer is Yes, and I don't know whether I want to talk about it. But I expect God has placed us together at this moment . . . I would say, very directly, that on one occasion Jesus, my companion, sent the Buddha to me. So

I received the Buddha, but he came from Jesus. That's all I can say.

GP: How did you know this?

Nicolls: In the same way I know you're sitting there. As direct as that. And afterwards I thought: 'The guys are all going to say *Oh yes*?' You know – I did philosophy! But now I don't have any doubt about it. .

GP: Were you in a specially prepared condition? (*I was thinking of fasting.*)

Nicolls: Yes, yes. But I wasn't prepared for the Buddha to appear.

We are now about to embark on a series of encounters with people who have absolutely no doubt about the existence of God because they have, in some sense, met Him or had an experience which they cannot account for in any other way. I have to say at once that this is not the conclusive evidence a believer might hope for; for while it is totally convincing to the subject who has had the experience, he or she cannot expect to pass it on in the same form to anyone else. Gripping it may be, but vulnerable to criticism.

Sometimes there are predisposing factors, like fasting, which can be seized on by the sceptic as accounting for the whole thing. More often than not, the experience is wanted or welcomed, sometimes deliberately sought by the subject, and so dismissable as wish-fulfilment. Very often it is clothed in the terms of a particular religious form which the subject has been studying – I saw the Buddha, I heard the voice of Christ, I felt the presence of the Holy Spirit – in ways which make the sceptic even more inclined to dismiss the experience as a psychological or neurotic construction out of the subconscious.

It is tempting, at first sight, to accept this explanation. Believers might say there is no reason why their God should not work through psychological processes and even neuroses. But I certainly did meet witnesses whose mental disorders and spiritual insights went hand in hand – though I must emphasise that I met many more who were normal and well-adjusted by any standards and whose experiences of the divine were quite as compelling.

Perhaps the most striking example of the former was Karen Armstrong, the author and broadcaster and ex-nun, whose life came to a climax with two extraordinary events: the moment when she apprehended God Himself in what turned out to be an epileptic fit, and the moment soon after when the autistic child she had been caring for found spiritual peace in the ritual of baptism. The trouble is, both cases could be seized on as demonstrating that God is the God of the mind that is sick. And Karen Armstrong had been told by her neurologist that people with her ailment – temporal lobe epilepsy – are often either very religious or very violent:

> When I have a *grand mal* attack, then I do see God. Dostoievsky describes it best in *The Idiot* – he was himself, of course, an epileptic. Suddenly everything comes together in a moment – everything adds up, and you're flooded with a sense of joy, and you're just about to grasp it, and then you lose it and you crawl into an attack. It's awful, because you've lost it. It isn't worth it, because you wake up feeling awful. It's easy to see how, in a pre-scientific age, an epileptic or any temporal lobe fringe experience like that could be thought to be God Himself.

Was there, then, any connection between Karen Armstrong's normal understanding of God and these great storms or the experiences people had under the influence of certain drugs? She thought it was true that certain things happened, physiologically, to people in deep meditation. But they could snap out of it at will, unlike those who were freaked out on drugs. It was a state of deep inner concentration, in which one had to avoid creating God in their own image and likeness:

> I think I would describe myself as a sort of positive agnostic; so that even though I think there is a God – and I am a very religious person – I am not sure that we can ever know very much about Him. If you think of *The Cloud of Unknowing*: 'Cast all your thoughts or preconceptions about God under a thick cloud of forgetting and approach Him as He is . . . My thoughts are not your thoughts, says the Lord, nor are my ways your ways. For as high as the heavens are above the earth, so are my thoughts above

your thoughts, my ways above your ways.' It almost seems as if, in our horrible society which is based on reason, aggression and intellect and overvalues the intellect so much, this other more contemplative frame of mind might in fact save the world.

Karen Armstrong lamented the intellectualized Christianity which burnt people at the stake for minute differences of dogma:

> This is God become politicised, God taken over by a purely human system of thought. I don't think God has anything to do with thinking or concepts or even images. It's much more a sense of mystery, in the fullest sense of the word. God's not a nut that you can crack and say: 'Eureka! I've found Him! Now I understand!' If we can understand God, He's not God.

This kind of God – the God of the Desert Fathers and the mystics – is going to be a disappointment to atheists who want to know what it is they don't believe in. Karen Armstrong doesn't know either; she can only say, in the ancient apophatic tradition: 'Not this – not that', but that there is *something* inconceivable there, she has no doubt:

> I think part of the trouble is that we expect God to conform to our notion of what is right and what is wrong. I think God, if we got to know Him, would be a horrible shock. The white-headed old man in the sky is out; but in a sense we do expect God to be like some kind of giant social worker who is going to sort everything out. But scripture says it is a terrible thing to fall into the hands of the living God. Perhaps things like autism or earthquakes when thousands of innocent people are killed overnight all add up to some really frightening part of the power, majesty and indeed beauty of God, and our little minds can't grasp this. You can say we might as well give up – He's an amoral God. I don't necessarily see that – just that His morals don't necessarily coincide with ours.
>   We're told that God is love, and again this tends to get melted down to some nice, warm, soupy glow with God as some lovely giant Mum or Dad. But love can be a very

frightening thing. I would say, if we try and think of all the aspects of love – love the raging fire, love the shock to the entire system, as well as the tender aspects of love – I think perhaps that's how I would define God. It's not a sort of mystical swooning, it's an electric shock. If a human being walked into God, he'd probably shrivel up. There's that moment in Newman's *Dream of Gerontius* where the soul sees God and says 'Take me away – take me away!'

So much for the theory that God is just a spiritual dummy to be sucked on at times of distress. And it would be as wrong, surely, to think of Him as a perpetual penal Lord. Perhaps part of the meaning of God's being personal is that, like a person, he is experienced as love and anger, darkness as well as light – that He *responds* like a person and does not go indifferently on His way. Or does He?

Robert King-Edward, a Scottish writer, admits that for many years he was the victim of anxiety neurosis, which ruined his health, his employment and with it his finances. God, he believes, was getting him so desperate that he would never say No when the moment of decision came; as it did one night in a Pentecostal church where the pastor urged him to 'appropriate his own salvation' by thanking Jesus for dying for him personally. Which King-Edward did. But the rewards have yet to show themselves:

I ask for blessing. I ask again and again, and of course there are blessings of a kind, but they're not the blessings I seek . . . The last few years have been very difficult years for me, and I haven't suffered in silence. I have complained a great deal to God. I protest a lot. I cry aloud to Him. I call Him names. I always repent, but I don't stop doing it. The fact of doing it is very therapeutic, but there's no obvious response. I do basically believe that God is love and I couldn't be a Christian otherwise. But the road He has made me walk for many years now has not been a road of love – it's been a road of discipline and obedience and of chastening. And that is virtually all I have known of God. I've no alternative but to follow this road, because I've committed my life to Him. And even if I could get out of it I couldn't allow myself to, because I know that what is outside God's kingdom is a great deal worse than what is inside it, as far as I'm concerned. He's made it in such a way that there is no escape. God has made me a prisoner.

Looking round King-Edward's stylish flat, I suggested rather brutally that he was a spoilt kid who ought to pull himself together. Well, that had been put to him by one or two of his friends: but only because they could not believe that God would be so cruel as to punish him so:

I can't see any way I'm responsible for my own afflictions. I have long accepted that it is of God. And you see there is a blueprint for it in the Bible – I think the Book of Job is a blueprint for suffering. It should surprise the Christian if he has *not* been required to suffer.

It was some days later that I was talking to Frances Young, the Birmingham theologian, who bears the very heavy cross of a severely handicapped child. We shall hear later how she has found light in that particular darkness, but I was interested to know whether she had had any experiences of the immediate presence of God – the kind of experience that her colleague Michael Goulder had said he lacked and found so rare among the clergy. Several, said Frances Young:

The first that was really significant was sitting in that chair over there one day, and I suddenly had a loud thought: 'It doesn't make any difference to Me whether you believe in Me or not!' And it wasn't a great emotional experience or anything like that, but it hit me between the eyeballs: it was a case of suddenly being put in my place and seeing all the wrestlings, doubts and struggles in a totally new perspective. And since that moment – I think you know we have our relapses – but I think the reality of God has not been seriously challenged any more. For years I recognised that no argument for the existence of God is a knockdown proof – that everything is ambiguous, everything is fifty-fifty – so how can you actually know God? That was part of the wrestling and suffering. You know scientists say that the flash of intuition is the thing that gives the key to the knowledge; and I've begun to see that experience as the moment of intuition which has enabled me to go on with the testing and questioning and argument, but still with a very profound assurance that in the last analysis it's not my mind that is going to settle the issue, and God really *is* there, and that at that moment I knew He was there.

On July 3rd 1984, Frances Young was ordained a minister in the Methodist Church. There were all sorts of reasons against it, notably the handicapped son, but what forced the decision upon her was once more an intervention whose source she is unable to question:

I was driving home and stopped at the traffic lights in Dudley, and suddenly I had another loud thought which was simply 'You should get ordained'. An extraordinary thing happened after that. I just don't know how I drove back – I'm not aware of the journey at all – I must have been on automatic pilot or something. I wasn't struck blind like St Paul or I would have landed in the ditch, which wouldn't have helped much. But during the course of that drive home from Dudley, I had the whole of my life laid out in front of me; and all its peculiar twists and turns which hadn't seemed to make very much sense suddenly fell into a pattern, as though this was all leading up to that moment and that conclusion. It was quite dramatic in its way. Next morning it didn't seem very realistic and I didn't say anything to anybody for several weeks. But then various other circumstances just happened and eventually I'm to be ordained.

To give evidence for the defence for a moment, it so happens that I am quite familiar with these loud thoughts myself and I have been forced to the same conclusion about their origin as Frances Young. To say they come from the subconscious is not much of an explanation, for if there is a God He is even more likely to be active there than He is in our noisy and selfish rational intellect. In any case, such loud thoughts do not come in a continuous stream. In my experience they are extremely rare and tend to appear long before the events to which they apply, after which they triumphantly click into place. One keeps trying to chase them out of the room, but like cats at supper-time they mysteriously reappear. It is this unwilled persistence that gives them much of their power. None of this can be demonstrated or transferred to anyone else, nor can anyone else persuade the experiencer that it is a delusion. In an odd way it is more real than a letter or a telephone call that could be shared.

'Loud thoughts' are only one form of the direct religious experience that many people claim to have had. A couple of years ago, I received a remarkable letter from a retired Cornish mining engineer in his late seventies who described to me – for the first time he had told anyone – an experience he had had some thirty years earlier:

One evening as I lay down to sleep I was suddenly aware of a most strange sensation of awe, fear, almost unbearable excitement, and I wondered if I was going to find myself in the next world. But of course I wasn't, and next morning I had to get up and get on with life.

About a fortnight later, a sunny afternoon in September 1948, I nodded off in an easy chair by the open window and awoke with the sun streaming down on my face – just enjoying doing nothing in particular, listening to the birds singing. But suddenly I became aware again of that strange mixture of fear and uplift entering my mind; and I sat there deeply puzzled for some minutes. Finally it became so insistent that I *had* to find out what it meant.

I walked up the passage to my bedroom, went down on my knees and asked for an explanation. As I did so, the glory of the universe shone before me – I was blinded by the dazzling white light. In my heart I flung my arms before my eyes, because I knew then that man could not look upon God and live. I was both terrified and yet uplifted – I can't explain it. I was shattered and then knew that I was a nothing. All my conceit and personal esteem vanished.

So great and awful was the Holiness that stood before me that I feared that it should ever happen again. But it completely changed my life. When I hear men in their folly say: 'You can't prove that there is a God!', I reply: 'You wait until He has taken half a step towards you and you are left in no doubt.' Why this happened to me, I can't understand. It may have been to arm and stiffen me for what was coming; for our world was about to collapse about our ears . . .' (*My correspondent then went on to describe the painful deaths of both his parents and the strength that his experience had given him*).

For several years past there has been a Religious Experience Research Unit attached to Manchester College, Oxford. It was founded by the distinguished zoologist, Sir Alister Hardy, directed by Edward Robinson (brother of the late bishop J. A. T. Robinson) and has been collecting and publishing records of such experiences. Sir Alister's basic thesis is that man's awareness of a power beyond himself is one of the basic drives in his makeup, as natural and undeniable as sex, and possibly the key to man's evolutionary success.

Associated with the Oxford Unit but working in the University of Nottingham is David Hay, a practising Roman Catholic, who has applied public survey techniques to the phenomenon. He found that if you just knocked on doors and slipped in a question about religious experience, about thirty-six percent of the adult British population would admit to having had one. The classic form of the question would be: 'Have you ever had a personal experience of a sort that made you aware of a presence or power – whether or not you call it God – which was different from your everyday self?'

But there is a cultural taboo on being frank in these matters. People, especially men, are afraid they will be thought stupid or mentally odd if they admit to such an experience. It is only when the researcher establishes confidence and can question in depth that it emerges – at least in Nottingham – that the positive response is more like sixty percent. Typically, says David Hay, it has a numinous or mystical quality:

A person is stepping out of the front door and suddenly they become intensely aware of some kind of presence. Commonly they don't see anything particularly, they don't hear anything, the normal sensory apparatus isn't involved; and yet they have this overwhelming awareness. And it's very typical for them to say the experience was more real than everyday reality. It's almost entirely the case that people feel very deeply moved and pleased that they've had the experience. It seems to give them some evidence that they belong in the universe. They relax into life, feel happier, find some kind of meaning if they didn't have it before, and if they are religious by nature they get an experiential confirmation of the theories they have previously held. If they are irreligious they tend to be not quite so hostile to religion. And the research shows that from a social point of view they become better citizens, more concerned about the community, more active on issues of social justice and things of that sort. The stereotype is that people reporting this kind of experience should be a bit crazy, introverted, cut off from reality and so forth; but again the research shows they score more highly on psychological well-being than other groups.

If this kind of experience is common to more than half the adult population, the obvious question is why everybody does not have it? If there is a God why does He not make the awareness of His existence available to everyone? For even if such experiences could be interpreted in a non-God way, it does not seem that everybody has anything like them. William James, the great American investigator of religious experience, felt that people were turned towards religion by a kind of sickness of the soul, a sense of being lost in the world, and that this led them towards experiences which would 'save' them. Freud took a rather similar view. But David Hay thinks that James was speaking from his own background as a New England puritan and that it is the irreligious person who is really handicapped:

> I think the results show pretty clearly that people reporting religious experience tend to be – perhaps because of their upbringing – rather more open psychologically than those who don't. People reporting 'peak experiences' (which include religious experience) are less likely to be uptight and straight-jacketed.

Another thing is that our cultural history is full of nasty stories – a lot of them true – about the way religious institutions have behaved in the past. A lot of us carry inside us a kind of nausea about that, and I think it closes people off from their religious experience. And another thing is the kind of metaphors utilised in a scientific society. I don't think people always realise that they *are* metaphors. If the man in the street thinks man is a machine and doesn't realise that is simply a metaphor scientists use for convenience, then that closes off the mind from looking at areas that religious people would think very important.

One of the things Hay is saying here is that up-to-date people refuse to submit themselves to experiences which cannot be explained in up-to-date terms, even if those terms are themselves only provisional. It is a bit like refusing to acknowledge great art as beautiful, because there is no scientific formula for explaining what that beauty is. David Hay is in fact baffled by the refusal of the literal-minded secular community to take seriously what is so obvious to him:

I am pretty impressed by what these people say. In fact it's so impressive, when you actually talk to a large number of people about this experience, listening to the depth of feeling and sincerity with which they talk about it, and the obvious sanity of them, that I can't but think we are onto something real here, and something that the culture we live in just totally ignores.

It seems to me that our culture ignores it because, provisional though they may be, the metaphors of science have delivered the goods – produced results – with spectacularly greater success than the metaphors of religion. Medical and agricultural research have achieved more in half a century than generations of prayer; and although it is proper to argue that prayer and research are not interchangeable, and that research has produced *ill* effects far beyond the capacities of prayer, nonetheless if it is results you want in physical terms, then religion comes a poor second at best. Religion *can* produce results, as millions who practise it will testify, but of a far less tangible nature. Does that mean they are less worth having? Why should it mean we cannot have both?

There are people who feel they have a relationship with God which is entirely practical, a series of prayers and answers. Such a one is Hilary Field, a glowing, enthusiastic evangelical who works for the Billy Graham machine. When she moved into her tiny house outside Bristol the garden was a mess and there was no mowing machine. So she held the problem up to the Lord, and by the end of the afternoon her neighbour had given her a load of lawn-turf in exchange for her rubble and offered her a mower for five pounds. In quick succession there followed a washing machine and a tumble dryer. Did that sort of thing happen to Hilary often?

> Yes, quite often. But if you read the Bible, God said time and time again that if you followed His commandments and loved Him, He would do His best to bless you back . . .
>
> But if you believe in a force for good, you believe in a force for evil and you have to start talking about Satan and where he comes into the picture. Since working for the visits by Billy Graham, I've had five car crashes – never had a crash before in my life. And my boss's house was struck by a thunderbolt and set alight.

I thought it was a bit much to thank God for the lawn mower and the washing machines while fobbing the car crashes off on the devil, but it did not seem odd to Hilary. Nor had she any doubt that the only true God was the Christian version: 'If you don't accept Jesus Christ in your life, then you do not know God.' God, she thought, would deal fairly with those who had never been told about Christ; and as for the Jews who rejected Christ, she was under the impression that more and more of them were turning Christian. For better or worse I fear it is not so and seems even less likely to be so among the Muslims; so I went off glad to have met someone who was convinced of God's activity in her life, but unhappy that His Son had become a test for admission.

Not that there isn't great subtlety in the second person of the Trinity. The human figure of Jesus enables the Christian believer to find God at work 'down here', in our terms, and not merely presiding 'up there', in His. Thanks to the Incarnation the Christian can claim to know what God has taught him and done for him in historic time, and through concepts like the Resurrection and the Eucharist can enjoy a personal relationship with the divine. Even though it is a heresy to separate Christ out from the Trinity and worship Him on His own, many Christians do in fact do so. They would be appalled at the thought of dealing directly with the awesome majesty of Jehovah, who in any case tends to get stuck in the Old Testament. It is as if, like Karen Armstrong and my Cornish mining engineer, Christians sensed in the Father a power that would blind them and shrivel them up; as if Jesus were not only as much as we needed but as much as we could take.

Is Jesus, then, a sort of extra to God? The Church has to say No – that He *was* God; though many people are confused at learning He was also the *Son* of God. Alistair Macdonald, the Scots folk-singer, thought he was a christian because he went to church on Sundays, worshipped God and 'brought Jesus into it'. But it was not until he 'saw Christ's example in others and asked Him into my life' (the classic evangelical commitment) that he felt he really knew God. Alistair admits that he was being asked to believe in something he had never seen personally, but he was able to make the leap of faith because of the effect he had seen in his wife and in others. And it was this which had made the scriptures convincing, not the scriptures in themselves which had won him over.

It seems, though, that (if there is a God) we can still take Him or leave Him as we like – that we are not going to be struck by lightning for disbelief. Alistair Macdonald reads his Bible otherwise:

Well, the record shows that some have tried that and *have* been struck by lightning. My choice is to believe that record or not, and I can't see why the record isn't so. I can't understand why any group of men should falsify the records in a way so difficult to swallow. If they were wanting to fool me they would have made the message an awful lot easier to take – because the promise is not an easy one. The Bible to me would be an awful lot easier if it were just a collection of warm wee stories for us to feel good. There is obviously something quite challenging between the covers of the Bible as I read it.

Certainly the atheist cannot accuse the Christian Church of having devised a dish of spiritual lollipops for its members to suck at. It is not, in fact, an easy way to find comfort; and I met witnesses who had only broken through to a belief in God and His goodness after a battering which had bruised their souls. For example, Anglican deaconess Shelagh Brown:

It happened at the time of the Charismatic Movement. I was very fed up because people were saying they had these fantastic experiences of God and being aware of the love of God, being thrown to the ground in prayer-meetings by the presence of God. And I was in a filthy temper with God because nothing ever happened to me. And one day I was so angry that I went into my kitchen and banged on the table in a filthy temper and said: 'It's no use to me you hanging on a bloody cross two thousand years ago if I don't know your presence now – utterly useless.' And I raged at God in a terrible temper. And then I stopped. And all I can say is that after that I had the most extraordinary deep sense of peace. And shortly after, when I was praying, it was as if, in my mind, I was being shown lots of truth. I had such an awareness of how things are that, eventually, I had to say: 'I can't stand any more of this – it's mind-blowing!' It was an insight into how things were, and the nature of things, and the nature of God – not caught up into a seventh heaven, it wasn't that, it was a pure mind thing and I couldn't take any more. And so I simply stopped . . .
    It isn't speakable, really. It was an awareness. It is like – I remember walking in the woods once – and as if there were angel's wings around me, though I don't believe in angels particularly. It's irritating when people talk about religious experience like that, but it is difficult to put an experience into words.

If there is a God, one would expect believers to be able to

meet Him in prayer, which, as holy people have developed it, is supposed to be not a one-sided pestering of God but a two-way dialogue. But as Shelah Brown experiences it, it is a strange dialogue in which one of the parties is endlessly silent, though His presence can be felt:

> The business of pouring out my heart to Him and saying: 'Lord, I'm unhappy – this is why' and spelling it out has to be balanced by sitting in total silence, quite still, aware of the fire, of the birds outside, of the breathing of my body. I suppose the thing I most want of all is to be known in the depth of my being and not to be alone there – to know that there is a presence that is aware of me.
>
> I was aware of it, curiously when I was at a Prom last year, listening to the most lovely music with somebody I greatly liked. And I was aware that somehow the experience I was having – of God together with me experiencing this beautiful music – was a far deeper experience than the presence of the man who was sitting by my side.
>
> To me prayer is almost the relationship itself. There is the business of talking, of seeming to get answers because I have a new dimension of understanding. But the loveliest thing of all is, I suppose, like being in love. You're not always yakking away, you are simply delighting in the presence of the other. And then you get furious with the other for failing to be what you would like the other to be. But then, as maturity comes, one realises one must allow the other to *be* the other; and that in the confrontation and the awareness is my way of growing; that the other is *not* me – the other is other – and I can therefore learn in the encounter. It's like that with God, I suppose.

This is so much the experience of mystics down the ages – this Otherness within oneself, with which one can enjoy a deeply personal relationship – that it simply does not ring true to dismiss it as a form of contemplating one's own navel. The sense of Otherness is too overwhelming, and in many cases – like Shelagh Brown's – the experience is not clothed in the sort of detail that would allow one to claim that a standard Christian tableau was being dutifully reproduced.

Insights of this kind are not by any means limited to people of Shelagh Brown's education.

One of the most impressive witnesses I met was a delightful old lady called Ethel Snowball, who lives in sheltered housing in Sunderland and does most of her religious thinking for herself. She went to Sunday school and Bible class in the same Church of England congregation she attends to this day. Sometimes she felt it let her down, and she shopped around the local churches 'without really knowing what I was seeking for', until one day she heard a preacher say something about 'the hand of God is there, and in trust you've simply got to put your hand into the hand of God – it's there for the taking.' Says Mrs Snowball:

I thought, that's what I needed instead of desperately seeking. I needed to be able to trust and think, well, He's done what He's done for me: I've got to take it that it's done. And from then on I began to feel I was getting somewhere. I was nearly forty years old and I'd been seeking from about fourteen. I was simply to leave things, stop thrashing about, and God would take care of them. I still fall away from it occasionally. I think I must have a wavering sort of nature. But I was taught just to leave things in His hands and to a great extent I do that.

You might expect from that an extremely traditional folk theology, but far from it. Mrs Snowball told me:

I think birth and death are very closely related. My friends at the House Group say 'You must be mad', but I say No – I've had a lot of illness at one time or another, and I've sat and thought about things. I think that a baby in the mother's womb is very comfortable in its own little world; and when we die it is like being born – we are pushed out of this world into something else, just as a baby is. Some babies can't wait to be born, other don't want to be born and they have to be pushed. A child could have fears as it's being born, as we fear death. I said, when you look at the welcome that child gets – nine times out of ten – when it is born – you can look for something similar when you are born into another world. That's the way I see it.

And Mrs Snowball sees something even more advanced theologically:

> My idea is that, in me as in you and everybody else, there's a bit of the Spirit of God; and I do try to think of that as being the real me . . . As I see it, it's like the raindrops: they come down and some go through the soil and some go to a stream and the stream goes to a river and the river goes back to the sea where the raindrops first come from. And I feel that little bit of me is a part of the Spirit of God, and that it will go back to that when we're all in accord – when the whole thing will be achieved. Then I'm a part of the Spirit of God, and that little bit of me, when I'm finished, goes back to form the Spirit of God. I think He's spread Himself abroad and He's in everybody. That's the way I see it. I may be wrong. But I can't visualise any judgment or anything like that.

A touch of pantheism, a touch of Quakerism, a touch of Buddhism, even. But underlying it all, a sense of something greater, underlying and overlaying the Sunderland grandmother. As we have seen, Ethel Snowball did not establish her relationship with God without a fight, and she is still quietly wrestling with Him to the astonishment of her House Group. But there came a point where she decided – not to swallow the doctrinal package whole, but simply to trust. In Rome I met a nun, Sister Monica Meehan, who had followed a more intellectual route to the same point:

> I definitely set out to find whether this was the real thing or not. I began to read and research in philosophy and history to prove to myself that there was a God, and I satisfied myself from the rational viewpoint. But rational religion is a limited experience, because I may believe in you, but to really have faith in you I must become vulnerable and trust in you. So there's an element beyond control and beyond rationality in faith.

Sister Monica first encountered that element during a religious retreat:

I looked up at the altar, and I can still see the colour: it was a light mauve, with light coming through, and somehow I experienced – yes – 'God, you are a reality', and I'll never forget this moment. It's just as vivid as I'm sitting here talking to you. That experience was deep, it was not something initiated by myself, but a deep conviction that God exists . . . And there was another time, it was within a church experience, the priest was saying a prayer in the sanctuary, and I can't explain why, but my life has never been the same since. It was a deep conviction there is a real presence here: a deep and very comfortable belief that God exists in this particular form. . .

GP: Do you think anybody could explain that away, arguing that it was slightly neurotic or something to do with the weather?

Monica: I think it could very easily be explained. But to explain it to me, nobody can enter my person – nobody can touch that sacred centre within me. It is something I don't invite people into because it is too secret and too real to me. I think anyone would have a hard time to convince me rationally or otherwise. I have experienced this God, I feel comfortable with this God. I am very open to reading and researching but at this moment in my life it would be very difficult to say, 'Well Sister, this was psychological – you were having an emotional experience out of touch with reality'. I would quietly listen, but I would not be convinced.

And having met both sides, I would be hard put to it to believe that Sister Monica was less in touch with reality than a professing atheist. She reads Sartre, works in the trendy field of communications, and is wholly convinced that God exists.

It may have occurred to some that I have been drawing more than usual upon the testimony of women witnesses – and it is supposed that women are susceptible to unrealistic promises. But I met women sceptics as well – Marghanita Laski and Iris Murdoch, for example – and made the pilgrimage to darkest Oxfordshire to visit an old acquaintance who is at the same time a licensed Anglican reader, a vicar's wife and an obsessive doubter. Alison Adcock's father was known to his friends as 'the pagan remains of a decent Presbyterian', and she says of herself: 'A parson's wife has got to believe in God, at least outwardly. You don't want to mess up your husband's career, do you?' But beneath the crust of self-deprecation there is an honesty about belief that challenges the easy answers. Mrs Adcock complains that she does not know what response to prayer means:

> I don't think I have experienced God at all. I think that's my trouble. I don't understand what they are talking about. By 'God' I mean the goodness and worth that I find in things that make the world into some sort of unity; and I want to serve that and promote that and enhance and be part of that. I think the universe is a harmony into which we can fit and in which there's a place for us. . .
>
> If you get a thoroughly materialistic society, a society which is just out for success in this world (which I think our society is beginning to look a bit like), then I think you've got a very nasty world in which people get hubris-tic. They think they're boss of the universe, and the only thing they've got to decide is which of them is going to be boss. They think they can do as they like, and they make a mess of things . . .
>
> A version of Christianity I very much dislike is the one that says God created the world for the benefit of us. I think we're here for the benefit of goodness. I can't stand the human racism of some people who think all these vast galaxies and aeons of time are here as a kind of Montessori kit to turn us into nice little creatures to live forever with God. The idea that anything that was big enough to live behind the whole of it would get any satisfaction from sitting round a table listening to the harps as we played them is just ludicrous.

So let Alison Adcock stand for the passionate apprehension that there is a principle of goodness behind the universe, but that we are most unlikely to establish any personal relationship with it whatever. What is to be made of these varieties of religious experience, ranging all the way from admiration of the abstract to a love affair with the Other within oneself, blazing visions of the unbearable, literal truth of the scriptures, a direct telephone line for questions and answers? To some it will seem obvious that there is 'nothing there' and that various people are trying various ways of making sense of the meaningless. To others it will seem equally clear that there is 'something there' but either something so far beyond us that we cannot define it, or at the same time so obliging that it offers itself to each according to his or her own condition. Julia Neuberger, one of the half dozen women rabbis in Britain, thinks the evidence is all around us but that it is not intellectual:

> In fact, I think most of the intellectual justifications for the existence of God are just so much nonsense. I don't have much time for a lot of that theological playing around, because it isn't convincing. I think the reason I believe in God is because it feels right. That's intellectually pretty rubbishy, but I can't put it better. I don't think it feels either comfortable or comforting most of the time. If I'm entirely honest about it and very personal, it feels as if there's some force outside myself and other people which I think doesn't control – and has given human beings free will – but has caused it all to come into being.

And then Julia Neuberger reflected precisely the spirit of challenge which had inspired this enquiry in the first place:

> I think the individual Jew will accept so much and then suddenly say 'Now look, God, that's enough! I'm not having that! Don't be absurd!' And will, in an odd way, wait for a reply. Whereas I think the average Christian is more likely first of all to make an approach through Jesus. (I know Jesus isn't in a sense an intermediary, but I think He's used as one.) The average Christian feels he can talk to Jesus and has in some way taken Him into his life; but it's not argumentative. I think there's a lot more respect, actually. I don't think Jews respect God much.

A tradition which I can see going back to Jacob wrestling with the mysterious stranger by the river and refusing to let him go without his blessing. If there is a God, the least He can do is to give us some clues about Himself, and there are more and more of us who are unhappy about clues left for us in Palestine almost two thousand years ago, perhaps growing cold. If we are to extract more knowledge of Him, we shall have to continue wrestling, even if it shocks those who are more than content with what they already have.

Ann Semple, a young teacher of religious studies in Glasgow, was a witness who impressed me enormously precisely because she had carried on that struggle:

> I come from the kind of background where a certain kind of conversion experience was required, round about the age of thirteen, and I duly had it. I didn't make the decision easily, and I didn't make it without a lot of fear and trembling at the time.
>
> My ideas about God and what it means to be a Christian have changed very dramatically since then. First and foremost, I think since God is a person with whom one is able to have a relationship, He has different kinds of relationships with different people; that the Gospel is an individual thing, and that people come to God in all kinds of different ways. Not all will have a conversion experience; and I think a great deal of psychological damage is done to people in being made to feel they must come to God in one particular way. That is clearly not the case.
>
> I was very scathing with older people who had doubts. I can see now that for everyone who calls himself a Christian there is a continual search, always a refining of our ideas about God. . .
>
> I think Christians are called first and foremost to be witnesses of their own experience of God – and nothing else. If we're talking about proofs of God's existence, it is not possible, I think, ever to argue anyone into the Kingdom of God. I don't think we operate on that kind of intellectual level. We operate as whole beings . . . Now that doesn't water down the Gospel or make it wishy-washy in any sense. I think you only have to worry about human beings when they cease to be interested in God. When they've stopped looking and when they've stopped searching.

GP: But how is it – and I keep asking this – that belief in God can be so optional?

Semple: I can't envisage any other possible situation. We would clearly be automata if we were forced to recognise God as He is. Without the possibility of choosing, there is nothing to our relationship. It's very much like marriage, isn't it?

As moral psychology this rings true, and the sceptic would say conveniently true. Again, the unbeliever finds himself at the impassable gateway: unless he is prepared to pay the admission of choosing to pass through it, he cannot get in to see the advertised show. The best he can do is to listen to the accounts of those who do pay to enter, and judge for himself its effects upon them. But for him there is always the possibility that the show is an illusion – that there is nothing really there. Let us next consult the professional critics.

4

Expert Witnesses

Sir Alfred Ayer, the distinguished philosopher, finds the search for God 'emotionally understandable but not intellectually coherent'. He also admits to lacking a sense of wonder at the world. Instead, he is just annoyed that there are certain questions about it he is not sure he can answer. What he refuses to do is to dress them up in religious stories and symbols:

> I think a symbol should admit of our being told what it symbolises; and if someone says what to me is a lot of gibberish, and then says, 'Oh, I didn't mean *that!*' then I want to ask them, 'What *do* you mean?' I'm not being presented with anything I can agree or disagree with until he makes a coherent proposition. I think it is a very reprehensible form of cheating for someone to utter sentences to which no meaning is attached, and then pretend that he has said something frightfully important . . . Anybody's meaning of what is asserted should in some way or other be testable.

Sir Alfred's positivist attitude towards what is or is not to be taken seriously is nowadays considered rather old-fashioned in the world of philosophy; but that does not in itself discredit it, and the attitude remains widely influential. Philosophy may seem a remote and irrelevant study to most people, but it trickles down into the worlds of teaching, literature, the mass media and even the Church, through the rank and file of the higher-educated, to affect the way quite ordinary people describe, analyze and explain their experiences.

To give one apparently trivial example, the late Dr C. E. M. Joad's catch-phrase 'It depends what you mean by . . .' made a whole generation aware that what they said often meant more or less – or something quite different – than what it appeared to mean on the surface; that language was not just the servant of thought and argument but often its master.

At the extreme, a statement is only meaningful (a proposition is only coherent) if it can be broken down into elements that can be observed and measured, connected logically, and repeated by anyone. That there is a cat in my garden is literally true because we all know what a garden is – and mine meets the tests – and we all know what a cat is, and there they are together. Even Sir Alfred Ayer would be satisfied.

But if I were to tell him that Jesus Christ had washed away my sins he would, I am sure, prove to his own satisfaction (if not mine) that I was talking comfortable nonsense – emotionally understandable but not intellectually coherent: it could not possibly be broken down into elements which could be observed, measured, logically connected up and repeated by anyone.

So is it untrue that Jesus Christ has washed away my sins? Millions of people would insist that it *was* true, and many of them would assert that it was true not only by faith but as part of their experience: they felt saved, they felt forgiven as a result of it, and it was an experience that anyone could share – anyone, that is, except people like Sir Alfred who insisted on applying to things of the spirit tests which were only applicable to things of the tangible world.

Most positivists would insist that they are not, in fact, so crassly materialist as to deny the reality of anything they cannot weigh, photograph and stamp on; but none, I think, would allow that 'There is a God in the Universe' was worthy to be called true in the same way as 'There is a cat in my garden'. And surely the believer must agree.

Some believers would argue that they were using the word 'true' in a different sense, and that God is a personification – albeit an inadequate one – of that which cannot be observed, measured, logically connected up or repeated to order. Yet other believers would insist that God's existence really is observable, though immeasurable, and that His manifestations are perfectly logical and endlessly repeated: that He is quite as real as the garden cat to those who are not determined to blind themselves to Him. But I must say, for myself, that I cannot stretch the language to that extent.

It seems to me, having heard the evidence so far, that if God's existence is true it must be so in the sense of being a probability (not a certainty) which, when grasped, does indeed make things coherent: they hang together, not because logic demonstrates they must, but because in that light you or I see that they do; and because subsequently they continue to do so, continue to make sense. May it not be an illusion? Yes, and that possibility would be important, too, if – as two or three of our witnesses have affirmed – there is a God who refuses to force us to believe in Him.

I tried it on Sir Alfred Ayer, that God would not be the God He is, if we could prove that He was. The response:

> I don't for one second understand it. First of all, it begs the question by supposing *that* He is. What you *want* to say is that your concept of God is such that His existence is indemonstrable – as if He were a Gödelian number. (Gödel proved that in any system of logic rich enough to contain arithmetic, there were propositions that couldn't be proved. These were propositions that settled themselves, though unprovable. He arithmetised the whole argument; and therefore a Gödelian number is a number corresponding to this sort of position.) Well, I think if you want to compare your deity with a Gödelian number, this is an extraordinary flight of fantasy in which I'm going to allow you to indulge.

It seemed to me that, although I still do not really understand what a Gödelian number is, I might have been getting somewhere. What I had to say was that although Sir Alfred was an extremely distinguished philosopher, there had been – and still were – other distinguished philosophers who believed in God: did he think it was somehow disreputable for them to respond to an apprehension which was not strictly logical?

> It is hard for me to say it is disreputable, because so many people whom I respect do so. But I am always astonished when they do. For instance, my successor at Oxford, Michael Dummett (who is a Roman Catholic) – he is an

extremely able philosopher in a very good tradition indeed. It mystifies me that he can believe what he does. But curiously, he divorces it entirely from his philosophy. So we have been friends for thirty years without this ever coming up between us.

A week or two later I found myself in Oxford, talking to Michael Dummett, and it seemed only fair to recite that passage to him. Professor Dummett, a large teddy-bear-like man, chortled happily and said Professor Ayer had never been able to understand what it was to have a religion, thus depriving himself of an essential ingredient of human experience; 'rather like someone who had never had a twinge of sexual feeling'. And he added:

> I don't divorce my religion from my philosophy at all. In fact, if I didn't have religious belief, I'm not sure that I should have the motivation to do philosophy. But it is a very natural mistake for Professor Ayer to make, because I have never written any professional philosophical articles touching on religion – I simply have never felt competent to do so . . . Let me say this about philosophy: in the analytical tradition I think we have recently come through what was probably a very healthy but destructive period. A lot was rightly pulled down that can't any longer be used in its original form. But until we have fashioned new conceptual tools, I don't think we can usefully tackle the problems that arise at the higher levels of the subject.

In other words, although Michael Dummett thinks religion is an essential part of being human, and as a Catholic finds the sacrament of the Mass important to himself, even he does not feel equipped to tackle religion as a philosopher. Does he ever wonder whether the whole thing may not be a gigantic, rather picturesque system of wish-fulfilment?

> No – I think that it would be rather more comfortable *not* to have a religious belief . . . Of course one could be an upright stoic. Nevertheless, there must be worse things than finding it difficult to live with yourself when you do wrong – any kind of discomfort fades. It can't in the end matter that much whether you stick to the principles you

have constructed for yourself. But for someone who believes in God, these are absolute commands, and it does matter very much. So I don't think the question of religion being a system of wish-fulfilment ever crosses my mind. It seems to me very obviously *not* a matter of wish-fulfilment.

In the course of the discussion Michael Dummett began to trace a parallel between God as the author and guarantor of morality and God as the author and guarantor of reality: if you believed in God, there was no gap between how God apprehended reality and its being so. This reminded me of the 18th century philosopher Berkeley, who thought things *were* because they were observed; and then had to account for their continuing to exist when nobody was looking at them; a feat he achieved by arguing that they persisted as ideas in the mind of God. As the clever rhyme puts it:

> And that's why the tree
> Continues to be,
> Since observed by Yours Faithfully – God.

Professor Dummett did not think this at all flippant:

I *am* saying something like that. I think that Berkeley's argument of the existence of God is a very profound one, though it is almost always ridiculed, as in that limerick. I think it is, if not the best argument, at any rate the one we can most fruitfully think about at the present time.

Needless to say, Professor Ayer has little use for it. But my purpose so far has been to show that equally distinguished professional philosophers can believe or disbelieve, and that no amount of proclaiming that God is beyond logical discovery will stop them arguing about Him.

Whether or not it is proper for them to do so is an intriguing question. It might appear that for many centuries Christian theologians and philosophers were virtually the same – one thinks of Augustine, Anselm, Aquinas, all the way to Descartes, Pascal and Berkeley himself. But that theology and philosophy were ever really the same is more debatable. Theologians were (and in many traditions still are) expected to serve the Church; but philosophers claimed to pursue the truth, wherever it might lead. Philosophers continued to draw extensively upon the pagan Greeks, but theologians looked primarily to scripture and christian tradition for their inspiration; and there are many philosophical problems, like the nature of mind and perception and how we know things, on which the Bible is silent. The 'philosopher of religion' may have reasons for taking seriously the sort of ideas that the pure philosopher would dismiss as improper, but he cannot afford nowadays to cut corners and make leaps which would discredit him in the eyes of his secular colleague. The secular philosopher is playing one game and must play it by the rules, but the religious philosopher has to combine two games and try to play each according to its own. He is always liable to be accused of cheating.

Over the centuries, philosophers who were Christians have felt that if the existence of God is true and if philosophy is the pursuit of truth, it must be possible to demonstrate the existence of God philosophically. The methods they have adopted fall into certain well-known groups which I shall now try to summarize briefly. If I do so with a certain lack of enthusiasm it is for two reasons: first, that each one of them has its defects and, second, that whatever appeal they may have for philosophers and theologians, they are not ultimately why most people believe in God.

Two important schools of thought surround the so-called Cosmological Argument (which tends to be favoured by Catholics) and the *Teleological Argument* (which tends to be favoured by Protestants). The latter is probably better known as the Argument from Design, insisting that the universe functions according to such exquisitely interlocking laws that there must be a design and therefore a Supreme Designer. We shall hear more about this shortly when we meet our scientific experts, but it must suffice to say here that it is an essentially 18th century view which has taken some severe knocks since. Far from demonstrating the perfection of the system, post-Darwinian science has revealed an enormous amount of accident, waste and chaos in the universe – indeed, it seems to be running downhill towards a point at which (to quote Bertrand Russell) 'nothing of the slightest interest will be happening anywhere'. The believer can reply that he has always been taught to expect the world to end some day; that God has made the only possible universe, whether we like it or not; and that mathematically, the universe is simply not old enough to have reached its present condition by chance. But the outcome of this argument is so dependent upon information which is still incomplete – and may never be complete – that it is hard to see how it can ever reach a safe conclusion.

More truly philosophical are the various branches of the *Cosmological Argument*, embracing the Causal Argument. Basically the reasoning is that since everything depends upon something before it, like an endless train of railway wagons rolling across the prairie, somewhere at the head of the Cosmos there must be a Divine Locomotive – itself caused by nothing, but necessary for everything – drawing it along. Since we must either begin with something or admit to an endlessness, either way the principle behind it all must be God. Why must it? demand the scientists. Why can't the universe itself be necessary, either given from the start or endless? And philosophers like Professor Ayer insist that it is nonsense to talk of God existing before time began. Time, in modern science, begins simultaneously with space (something with which the 5th century St Augustine of Hippo agreed). But if so, where/when was God before the Big Bang? If there was anything, why call it God?

The great mediaeval theologian St Thomas Aquinas drew in much of what I have outlined in his Five Ways of proving the existence of God:

1. From Motion: There must be a prime mover of the cosmic train.

2. From Causation: There must be a cause of all causes which must itself be uncaused, or it could never have started the rest off.

3. From Necessity: There *must* be a self-sufficient First Cause of the Universe because we cannot give a satisfactory explanation of the world without it. For everything to be possible one thing, God, is necessary.

4. From Example: In order for us to have the ideas of higher and lower, better and worse, there must be an

ultimate Perfection in the Universe. One form of this argument is that our awareness of Moral Good points to the existence of God.

5. From Design: alias the Teleological Argument, which as we have seen is rather at the mercy of science.

At the risk of introducing yet another technical term, there is a further classic argument for God's existence, attached to the Cosmological family, devised by St Anselm of Canterbury about the end of the 11th century and still of considerable fascination to philosophers like Michael Dummett (though naturally Sir Alfred Ayer will have none of it). This is the *Ontological Argument* (the argument to do with the nature of being), and it goes like this – simple but slippery:

> If, by 'God', we mean 'that than which nothing greater or more perfect can be conceived', then such a being must logically exist, because without existence it could not be the greatest and most perfect.

Instantly one feels there must be something wrong with the argument, though it is not so easy to explain why. Surely God *must* be incomparably the greatest and most perfect being anywhere: so the rest follows.

But wait a minute! Are we not saying, '*Since* God exists as the greatest and most perfect being – therefore He exists', which is rigging the result in advance? I might as well say that anything I care to talk about must exist – centaurs, Martians, motor-cars that never go wrong. Just because I have a beautiful idea in my head, it does not follow that there is something that corresponds to it outside. Existence does not depend upon what we can imagine, but upon what can be experienced. So the simple logic of the argument collapses. And yet this does not prove there is *no* God, and one is still oddly intrigued by the proposition that something possessing absolute greatness and absolute perfection might exist. At the very least the proposition seems to express – seeks to confirm – a belief arrived at through one or more other routes. No proof of God has ever been totally convincing, or there would be no atheists. Nor has any disproof, or there would be no believers.

It is perhaps surprising that atheism has not had a much longer history. Atheists seem to have been rare in the ancient world and even rarer in the Middle Ages: many of those who were denounced as atheists were simply applying human reason to render unnecessary some of the magical interventions attributed to God, but they seldom if ever denied the existence of a Supreme Being. It was disillusion with the Church, its doctrines and personnel that really started the rot among the intellectuals. The English Deism of the 17th and 18th centuries allowed of a universal natural religion, presided over by a God of Reason and Natural Order, but scornfully rejected all miracles, prophecies and superstitions including those peddled in the Bible. The Church of England – as usual – tolerantly digested the heresies; but transplanted to France and tended by thinkers like Voltaire and Rousseau, they developed into the anti-clerical and even anti-christian movement that flared up with the French Revolution. The Catholic Church – not for the first time or the last – made the mistake of aligning itself with the forces of political and intellectual reaction.

It is not really until the 19th century, perhaps the 1830s, that we begin to find total and explicit atheism. From our point of view the key figures are probably Feuerbach, Nietzsche, Marx and Freud. Feuerbach, for a time a student of Hegel, began as a theologian but became convinced that the idea of God was incompatible with a liberated philosophy for the human race. He saw religion in what today we would call psychological terms: God was no more than a projection of the human will. The very concept of the Incarnation – God became flesh in the man Jesus – was the key to what had happened: Man *was* God, and in loving God Man was really loving himself.

Nietzsche (who read Feuerbach as well as the pessimistic Schopenhauer) was viciously anti-christian. To him Christianity was not merely false, it was 'the one great curse, the one great intrinsic depravity, the one great instinct for revenge for which no expedient is sufficiently poisonous, furtive, underground and petty . . . The Christian concept of God is sick, corrupt, the contradiction of life'. For Nietzsche the Christian virtues added up to a sickness which perverted the destiny of man and sought to frustrate the will of Superman.

Freud was an atheist before he became a psychoanalyst, deriving his attitude from Feuerbach and detesting religion almost as vehemently as Nietzsche did. To him, belief in God was the festering result of a neurotic and immature relationship with one's father. Freud delivered some shrewd blows at theologians who stretched the meaning of God to cover the vaguest of abstractions or who argued in a half-religious way that we ought to carry on as if religion were true, on the grounds that it was good for society.

Marx thought it was definitely bad for society, because it distracted attention from changing the real world by pointing to an unreal hereafter. Man looked to Heaven for a superhuman being and found nothing there but the reflection of himself. 'Man makes religion, religion does not make man' wrote Marx, but he did *not* go on to say – as many people suppose – that religion was an opium *for* the masses, concocted and administered by the ruling class. What Marx *did* say was explained to me by Gerry Cohen, Reader in Philosophy at University College, London:

> He actually said four things: he said religion is the sigh of the oppressed creature, the heart of a heartless world, the spirit of spiritless conditions, the opium of the people. If you take these together, they have some implications which might be missed if you take just the last one.
>
> Because the opium of the people suggests that priests give it to the people to keep them quiet; but actually it's very important in the Marxian view that religion is the creation of the people themselves – it's the sigh of the oppressed creature. Now this has the consequence that there could not be a Marxist justification for an anti-religious state policy, since according to Marx religion only flourishes if there's a lack of spirituality in secular life itself. A flourishing religion as in Poland would be a mark of failure in secular life.
>
> In the true view of Marx, there's no point in persecuting religion, because as long as secular reality is deficient, it will keep on erupting again. Also there's no need to persecute it to make it disappear, because the course of history will bring about an appropriately spiritual secular

reality which makes religion unnecessary. So it's a real perversion of Marxism for East European states to be hostile to religion in the way they are.

But could Marx really have used so unmaterialist a concept as the spiritual, I asked? Gerry Cohen thought it meant a deep caring about other people in one's work and daily life, 'so that you don't have to go to Church in order to express it, because the caring is taking place from day to day.' Well, if that is all Marx thought spirituality was about, he had a misshapen idea of religion.

Gerry Cohen describes himself as an agnostic who isn't convinced that God doesn't exist. He is about ninety-five per cent sure, but finds it hard to go all the way in believing that what has engaged the energy and commitment of so many fine and reflective people throughout history is an illusion. On the whole he thinks that theodicy – the attempt to reconcile the existence of God with the presence of so much unnecessary suffering and evil – just does not work. But as to whether religion has done so much harm as to discredit itself:

> How do you tell whether religion's been harmful? You have to try and imagine human history without religion, but that's absurd. You might as well ask whether government has been harmful. Religion has been too integral to human existence to imagine what things would have been like without it. It's been there whenever there's been good and whenever there's been evil. It's been on both sides. As for today, it's my uninformed judgment that it's playing an increasingly progressive role in the world, and that religious people are increasingly exercised by the plight of oppressed and dispossessed people all over the world in ways they used not to be.

So it is at least debatable that belief in God has been a disaster for the human race; and when one looks back over the legacies of our four key atheists it is very hard to conclude they have been a blessing. The Feuerbach-Nietzsche line leads relentlessly to Hitler; Marx to Lenin, Stalin and their heirs; while the answer to Freud lies in Jung, who remarked that of all his patients above the age of thirty-five there was not one whose problem was not that of finding a religious attitude to life. Far from religion being neurotic, it was the absence of religion that led to neurosis. None of these dismissals proves that there is a God, and Freud's acid criticisms of the pseudo-religious are justified. But surely we should hesitate before throwing out the baby of faith with the dirty bathwater of the Church.

Is there any point at all, though, in arguing about the existence of God? Might it not be best to say that since the truth of His existence is not of a logically provable kind, one should simply go along with it if belief is part of the culture (since one will probably be happier that way), and not if it isn't?

There are two objections to this apart from the conscientious one that it is not intellectually honest. We are in a transitional culture which does not seem sure whether it believes or not. And there are philosophers who contend that we *can* argue reasonably about God, up to a worthwhile point, even if not all the way.

For example, there is Richard Swinburne, Professor of Philosophy at the University of Keele. The key to his argument about God (*The Coherence of Theism* as his book calls it) lies in the distinction between *deductive* proof and *inductive* proof:

> Any argument starts from certain premises – certain things we can take for granted – and moves from them to a conclusion. A deductively valid argument is one in which the conclusion is made inevitable by the premises. You can't assert the premises and deny the conclusion without contradicting yourself. But an inductive argument is one in which the premises make the conclusion probable, or at any rate add to its probability.

It seemed to me that if deduction produced conclusions that were unavoidable, while induction produced conclusions that were only probable, then deduction was the more reliable – though less interesting because it could not reveal anything that was not built in from the start. Deduction might clarify, but it was essentially uncreative.

Now we have already toyed with the notion that religion has different standards for what is true from science or history. But Professor Swinburne does not agree. He thinks it is fundamentally reasonable to believe in God, although the sad fact is that this escapes many people, and for three reasons. First, they do not appreciate what evidence really is. Second, 'life is a lot easier if you don't have big metaphysical convictions' (i.e. people are spiritually lazy). Third, 'Religion has sold itself badly'. Nevertheless evidence is there, of many kinds, and the one Swinburne stresses most strongly is the fact of science itself: that our world is an orderly world. The Professor then embarked on a sample argument:

> Objects of all kinds behave in totally predictable ways, day after day. Take Newton's law of gravitational attraction: each particle, everywhere in the universe, has exactly the same property in this respect. Now this is a quite extraordinary phenomenon. There could so easily have been a totally chaotic universe in which things had different properties.
>
> Surely, when a rational man finds all the cards in the pack are the same or all the flowers in some neighbourhood are of exactly the same species, he says to himself 'There must be an explanation of this'. And the very nature of explanation is to look for one thing that explains many. And that is what the enquirer must do when looking at the universe. He must say: 'I can explain why everything in the universe behaves the same if it has one being who created it and gave it that power'. And that, I think is an obvious step to God.
>
> Now I'm not saying we can give a deductively valid proof of the existence of God. But there's very little in life we can give deductively valid proofs of. Science can't give you a deductively valid proof that the sun will rise tomorrow, let alone that Einstein's laws are the true ones. Science uses inductive, not deductive, inference.
>
> I think it was very unfortunate that people asked the question in the form 'Can we prove the existence of God? No. Therefore there is something disreputable about God'. But the point is, most of the things for which we produce reasonable arguments in ordinary life – and in science – are not things we can prove in this sense. But they are things we can give good inductive arguments for.

I went into the philosophy of religion with this deep conviction, that it had missed something very important here – because of a failure to understand what were the true standards for assessing arguments for the existence of God. They were not 'Are they deductively valid?' but 'Are they inductively cogent?' That is to say, do they make their conclusion probable?

What I extract from this is that the *inevitability* of there being a God is not built into the evidence we have, the universe. But that evidence does point towards a very high probability that there is one, and if we accept that conclusion it makes the evidence coherent – it hangs together in that light. As Professor Swinburne puts it:

A whole mass of things is made sense of by a more simple entity or general pattern of behaviour, which makes the detailed phenomena probable; and this is the characteristic of good, inductive inference in science . . . Well, if that's the right way of making sense of the universe on a smaller scale, it ought to be the way of making sense of the universe on a larger scale, and that is what I suggest the natural theologian ought to be doing.

The argument for the existence of God which I gave you has as its premise the order of the universe. I don't think on its own it makes the conclusion probable. But together with various other phenomena I think it makes a case – indeed, to my mind, a compelling case – for saying that the existence of God is more probable than not.

One of the great failings of the philosophy of religion in the past was to suppose that if something didn't conclusively prove by itself the existence of God, then it ought to be thrown away because it had no part in a case. But we don't argue that way in science. We think all sorts of detailed phenomena, which of themselves don't make probable any big theory, nevertheless adds each its own weight to that theory. Together, they make the theory probable. And I think it's like that with God.

I noticed that Professor Swinburne seemed to put individual religious experience (of the kind I reported in my previous chapter) fairly low down on the scale of evidence. He agreed that one had to be more careful with them than with experiences that could be publicly shared by others. But there was no reason why a rational man should not come to rely on his religious experience. The rational man was the credulous man: that is to say, he must start by believing his experiences as they seemed to be, in the absence of evidence to the contrary, otherwise he would never believe anything about the world. 'If you say, "I won't believe that until somebody produces further evidence for it – and then further evidence again"', we could never even get started.' And Richard Swinburne made an additional point which is really fundamental to the thousands of words in this whole enquiry:

> All human talk about God is by analogy. In saying He is very good, very powerful and so on I mean that His goodness is like what we recognise as goodness, only it's slightly different . . . It is our understanding of the world which has led us to a notion of a God who is its source; but serious reflection on what it is to be the source of the world can only lead to the realisation that He has aspects which go so far beyond human understanding that all we can do is bow down and worship.

This being the realm of philosophy, it is barely necessary to say that Swinburne has been energetically opposed; in particular by J. L. Mackie of Oxford whose mockingly titled *The Miracle of Theism* is largely devoted to knocking Swinburne down, with the conclusion, 'The balance of probabilities, therefore, comes out strongly against the existence of God'.

Swinburne seems confident, however, that science is on his side – or at any rate, not against him. A scientist who takes the same view, from a rather original standpoint, is Dr Rupert Sheldrake. Dr Sheldrake is a Christian and a plant biologist, who does most of his practical work in India. When he is in England he lives in the unexpectedly charming town of Newark which little knows, I suspect, that it is harbouring a scientific heretic who believes that plants and animals can 'tune in' to the experience of their predecessors ('A sort of cabbages' Old Boy Network or a cabbage collective memory', he explained to me) and that what makes an elephant an elephant is not some genetic programme woven in DNA but a designing principle which he calls 'formative causation'. It sounds remarkably like the will of God:

> Formative causation is a principle in the universe which gives things their shapes, forms, orders and patterns. When you have a house being built the building materials are obviously necessary, then the energy that's involved, but there's a third element which is the plan of the house. Now that plan is what gives the house its form. And I think in the natural world we have exactly the same thing . . . The genetic material, the DNA, enables plants to make the right kinds of chemicals and proteins, but just having the right chemicals won't give you the right shape of organism, any more than having the right kinds of bricks will give you the house you want. You still need to have this formative principle at work as well.
>
> Mechanistic biologists – people who believe that living organisms are nothing but inanimate machines – feel very satisfied with this idea of a genetic programme. But DNA is just a chemical that gives rise to other chemicals, it doesn't really explain all these things. The genetic programme is the way in which the mechanist smuggles in the vital principle or the life force and the intelligent guiding principle of design – smuggles it in by illegitimate analogy with a computer programme. You'll notice the programme presupposes the programmer, a conscious intelligence which actually designs the programme. The computer by itself can't do anything intelligent or impressive. So you also need this designing, organising principle which has a goal or purpose . . . In the thinking of the conventional biologist the computer programme is the DNA. The explanation seems satisfying until you realise it is a fraud.

Rupert Sheldrake is amazed that his colleagues don't share his sense that there is something mysterious, transcendent, almost occult behind the world of science. What *are* these things called the laws of nature, believed to underly the entire natural realm and everything we experience in it? You can't see them, they are not matter, and although they can be represented on paper they remain in the realm of ideas. Sheldrake is intrigued by the Indian idea of the world as 'the dream of God'. But does he not agree that scientific discovery is steadily cutting God down?

> I think what cuts God down is the idea that we know all the answers, and that we've got it all buttoned up in a few mathematical formulae. Some scientists think we under-stand more or less all we need to understand, and that another fifty years of research will fill in the gaps.
>
> I think if we really look at nature in an open-minded way, it helps us to see how extraordinary, how mysterious and how wonderful it is. What cuts God down is the blasé reaction 'It's just a gravitational field – it's nothing but electromagnetism!' – as if we really understood what a gravitational field was or how it got there in the first place. And living organisms – 'Oh, they're just chemical machines!' It takes away the wonder of them, you see. That's what cuts God down, not the discoveries of science, not the attitude of enquiry into nature.

Perhaps it is worth noting that Rupert Sheldrake is one of the life-scientists, concerned with living organisms, and that the present glamour-boys of science – the theoretical physicists – tend to regard them as rather old-fashioned and romantic, not yet arrived at the enlightenment of realizing that ultimately it all comes down to the magic formulae of physics. But what Sheldrake is suggesting is that if you are determined not to see God, determined not to raise your eyes from the brute facts at your feet to the horizon beyond them, then of course you will not see God.

I detected a slight raising of the eyebrows on the face of Professor Paul Davies, at Newcastle, when I confessed I had come to him from Dr Sheldrake. Professor Davies is up at the spearhead of the New Physics, where they have little use for morphic resonance among the cabbages or formative causation among the elephants, and where the cry is now 'The universe *is* a free lunch!' – which, I should explain, is an adaptation from the old American folk-wisdom 'There is no such thing as a free lunch', i.e. you can't get something for nothing. According to the New Physics there is not even a role for God as the Creator who lights the blue touchpaper of the universe and stands clear. Says Paul Davies:

> We can now conceive of the universe bringing itself into being automatically, spontaneously, without any prior cause. It has its origin in quantum physics. Previously we always thought that every event that occurred must have some cause that came before it. But when we go to microscopic phenomena and look down among the atoms, we find events that occur without any apparently well-defined prior cause. We can find particles that just pop into being out of nowhere for no apparent reason. There's a sort of anarchy at the sub-atomic level.
>
> Now of course the universe is big and I'm talking of little things. We believe that the entire physical universe came into existence in the so-called Big Bang about eighteen million years ago; and during this Big Bang the universe was very, very compressed and so we can talk about these quantum effects at a very early stage. Because the quantum effects allow structures to come into being without well-defined prior causes, we can therefore conceive of the idea of the universe coming into being without any prior cause. It indicates no surprise any more.
>
> *GP*: But how did anything arise out of nothing in the first place to go bang?
>
> *Davies*: You see, people have this terrible misconception about the Big Bang. They like to think of it as an exploding lump of something, sitting in a pre-existing void. But that's not at all the picture the professional cosmologist has. The Big Bang represents not just the coming into being of materials, but also the coming into being of space and time – and this is a most important point. It means there really *was* no 'before'. We can't talk about the explosion happening somewhere, because it represents space *coming into being* and time *coming into being*.

Clearly things are getting very rarified, because if the Creation/Big Bang was the moment when time was born as well as space, then we can no longer think of time as the eternal backdrop. And if you still insist on a Creator God, He must be not only ouside space but outside time as well (as Augustine of Hippo foreshadowed). If you further accept the physicists' contention that the universe set itself going – appearing uncaused as a 'quantum event' – then there is little for God to do but lie behind the physical universe supporting it in some timeless, incomprehensible way. Whatever that is, it is not the traditional idea of the personal, caring, intervening God.

However, Professor Davies can see room for a rarified God of this kind, and it has distant echoes of Berkeley mixed up with the New Physics. One of the fundamental things about quantum physics (which concerns these tiny, unpredictable, uncaused events) is that the mind of the observer plays a central role: 'The observer is at the centre of the stage determining part of the action . . . The true reality can't be separated from the observer.' Further, when we look at the laws of physics, it is hard to see how they could be very different from what they are and observers still be able to exist in the universe. Minute changes in those laws would spell disaster for life. So, says Davies:

> It is apparently a remarkable fact – and by no means logically inevitable – that the laws of physics have been organised in just such a way that observers like you and I are here to wonder about it all. So through quantum physics and through this fine tuning of the laws of physics, we seem to find that observers – and hence mind – appear to be part of the action. We're not just here for the ride. We actually seem to be (as it were) written into the laws of physics.

Hopefully – on behalf of the believers – I wondered if we were not, after all, getting back to the Old Testament Creator; or at least to reinstating the notion of the universe as an idea in the mind of God? Paul Davies was not going to be *that* old-fashioned:

> I don't think that sort of metaphor is really necessary. At least for me this collection of laws of physics suggests that there is some meaning behind existence. Whether or not

one wants to say it's God is a rather personal thing. Studying the laws of physics, we find that our existence here is a fundamental fact, and I don't think the laws of physics are just some accidental set. I think they seem to be very special, highly contrived, but that's as far as science can take us . . . But I'm convinced there is an element of design in some suitable generalised sense, and the universe isn't just a gigantic accident.

When I put it to him that there was only one possible set of laws for the universe, Creator or no Creator, because of the imperatives of logic and mathematics, Davies surprisingly disagreed:

People believe that, but I don't for technical reasons. It seems to me that one can look at the laws – at least as we understand them at present – and one can conceive of different logically consistent sets of laws which would give us very different universes. Indeed, most of my time and the time of my colleagues is taken up with playing with alternative laws and seeing what you get. So I find it remarkable when people say there can only be one logically consistent set of laws. If that is the case, one doesn't really need a God at all, because these laws would (as it were) bring themselves into being. I don't believe that.

That does not mean to say Professor Davies feels obliged to embrace traditional religion, which he finds too dogmatic, too intolerant of new ideas. But he does find a mystical content in science and he thinks there will always be something called God, not to run the world or to answer prayers or light the blue touchpaper, but underpinning the laws of physics: 'I believe there'll always be some room for God, but not the sort of God that most people have in mind, I'm afraid.'

To me, the most intriguing thing to emerge from the conversation with Professor Davies was the apparently necessary link between the universe and 'observers like you and me'. If we were not here, neither would it be here. Whatever the professor may think, I find this not too far from the Genesis picture of God creating man to enjoy the world, or (in modern scientific terms) 'the anthropic principle' – though this is unpopular with

environmentalists who think man has become altogether too
conceited about his own precedence over other species. John
Bowker, of Lancaster, cited the view that 'the reason why the
universe had to be so immense is that it was all there to produce
us . . . It is of the kind it is because it was going to produce
conscious life which would work back upon it and participate in
it', which obviously implies a designer with that intention.
Bowker maintained that the emergence of life as one chance in a
billion billion was no longer credible: it now looked so predict-
able under the circumstances as to approach certainty.

John Polkinghorne was Professor of Mathematical Physics at
Cambridge University until 1979, when he decided to stand
aside for the younger generation and enter the ministry of the
Church of England. Not surprisingly he believes in God as the
sustainer of the universe, though it is as a scientist as well as a
Christian that he views the 'free lunch' theory with some
suspicion. It just might be possible for the universe to have
come out of a vacuum, but it is an abuse of the language to call a
vacuum nothing. It is a 'very complicated churning, fluctuating
sort of object, the exact nature of which depends on the laws of
physics themselves'. John Polkinghorne appreciates the
'anthropic principle', even allowing for the existence of other
conscious beings in the universe, and he connects it with the
Christian doctrine of God becoming Man in Jesus Christ 'a
participant in this strange world that He had made – that He
isn't just a benevolent spectator looking down on human
suffering'. From which, I suppose, one might argue that the
timeless God contrived the universe the way He did precisely in
order that He might have a way of breaking out of timelessness
by way of Incarnation.

Polkinghorne was a good transition from the world of the
secular philosophers and scientists into that of the theological
experts. John Bowker had already told me he thought relations
between the two sides were a great deal more constructive than
they used to be – since both now realized that their accounts of
the world were always approximate and provisional. Now
Richard Harries, who is Dean of King's College, London,
assured me the notion that science was reasonable while religion
was not was very much a hangover from a century ago:

I agree it is still part of popular consciousness. But the fact of the matter is, a great number of very distinguished scientists believe in God. Certainly at a place like King's I suspect a higher percentage of science students believe in Him than some of the people from the Arts departments. I think there would be a greater degree of scepticism among, for instance, people reading History. People who have to handle documents and are used to everything being relative find it increasingly difficult to subscribe to something absolute. The great difficulties in believing don't come from science at all, but from other areas altogether.

Which, as an example of what actually happens instead of what everyone thinks must happen, is extremely interesting. It suggests that many people make their judgments upon religion not on the basis of the arguments, but on what they conclude about human nature.

The Reverend Don Cupitt, Dean of Emmanuel College, Cambridge, is a name to make traditional Anglican flesh creep. The handsome, articulate telly-don has turned out a succession of books and films bringing him closer and closer to a God so abstract and stratospheric that many Christians maintain he has no God up there at all. Dean Cupitt insists that he is simply trying to clear away the superstition and dross and articulate what the ordinary, simple Christian really believes; that he is trying to disentangle the strictly religious meaning of God from the old metaphysical picture of Him as a super-person controlling the world. He makes remarks like:

God is a necessary idea for us to have. God is the religious ideal. God is the guiding star by which we live . . . My idea of God is something with which I confront the world; it's not something that I read off the world . . . I don't think in terms of the 'existence' of God at all . . . God is more like an ideal, or the sum of our values, or the aim of our lives, a goal that we live by. So that the idea of existence is inappropriate. It would be better to say that God is eternal, timeless, not in the world of fact at all.

To a good many people, for God not to be in the world of fact would render Him a fiction. But that would not be fair to Don Cupitt, who was one of the *Myth of God Incarnate* group, a group which by 'myth' was not intending to say 'untruth' but rather 'symbolic story'. Don Cupitt argues:

> The whole of human knowledge consists in applying patterns and symbols to the world. The world has no structure of its own. The only structure there is in any of our experience is one that *we* put in; so it's *we* who give all meaning to the world. Every branch of knowledge nowadays is a human construction, human symbolism, a human attempt to impose pattern upon the flux of experience. So all our knowledge implies projecting myths – physics as much as religion . . . I choose Christianity as my life-project; I live by it. We must live by something, because we won't become human otherwise.

Don Cupitt, of course, is an existentialist. To him, religion is essentially a subjective way of shaping one's own life, and a religious truth only becomes so by being appropriated and made part of one's selfhood. Is there then nobody to respond to our prayers? It took me a bit of a struggle to get the answer:

> Well, you can't any longer, in modern conditions, think of things 'out there'. I don't believe there is *any* objective reality at all in that sense . . .
>
> *GP*: But how can there be a God if there isn't anything there for us to apprehend, even mistakenly?
>
> *Cupitt*: Because the idea of God on my account is non-factual. It's a transcendental ideal which gives worth to our lives. But God is not factual. If God were made factual, that would be a case of what Scripture calls idolatry.
>
> *GP*: You say God is non-factual. Does this mean there isn't a God?
>
> *Cupitt*:   The question concerns the *reality* of God and His power in shaping our lives. The difference between a person who believes in God and a person who does not believe in God is that in the case of the believer, his idea of God plays a part in shaping his life. Whereas a person who does not believe in God can't see how to use the idea, it has

no power for him . . . So the question of the reality of God is the question of His power in your life, not the question of whether He exists as a being. Because, if God existed as a being, He would be an idol, a graven image.

I must confess I do not see why an objectively existing God should have to be described as a graven image; and I would have been happier if the Dean had simply answered Yes or No to my question instead of substituting a different one. But then I appreciate that if a philosopher gets what he regards as a meaningless question, one should be grateful to him for answering another as near to it as he can find. Don Cupitt is, I suppose, the theologian of Paul Davies's timeless God, and I think one can see quite clearly the sort of God he is trying to make.

What cuts him off from the average believer (who would be surprised to be told that it was he or she who *gave* meaning to the world, rather than discerned it already there) is Cupitt's refusal to believe that the timeless could have thrown a bridge across into time and space and could somehow be active there. Many liberal Christians would accept that we have constructed a myth – a symbolic story – about God; but that it is based upon nothing but our desires and aspirations does not ring true to them. However, we have not heard the last of Don Cupitt, either here or elsewhere.

In the academic tradition of giving dong for ding, Cupitt has been answered in print by Professor Keith Ward, a colleague of Richard Harries at King's, London. But equally true to tradition, Professor Ward was not inclined to attack Cupitt personally:

I would like to stress that I very much respect the things he says, and feel the force of them. I don't think this is some empty de-mythologising: I think there are some very good reasons for it. But Don believes we have gone away from the view of the universe as rational and purposive and having an objective value in it. I must say my experience is the opposite of that. The more I talk to physicists and to younger philosophers, a significant number (though not all of them) are saying the whole tradition of philosophy has been in favour of the view that the universe is, at its heart, spiritual, valuable and purposive. This is an objective statement about the way the world is – that the basis of reality is a spiritual basis. I think that Don is allied to a dying school of thought. Up-to-dateness is not the criterion of rationality, but I do not find that – as he says – there is a great tide of secularism flowing over the world so that belief in an objective God is becoming more difficult. I doubt very much whether that's true.

Keith Ward insists that some of the most influential philosophers of our time – Wittgenstein and Whitehead, for example – though not conventional Christians, have been religious people and completely opposed to Sir Alfred Ayer's positivism. All the most influential schools of philosophy in the world today, like the Australian materialists, are against positivism and are making 'big metaphysical claims about the nature of ultimate reality – so that's a straw in the wind'. Even though, for the record, Professor Ward does not really approve of Australian materialism, whether or not it has anything to do with cans of chilled Foster's lager.

Ward agrees with Swinburne that while the classic proofs of God cannot produce the Deity out of a hat, they form a cumulative case which 'points towards the existence of a God'. He is impressed by Anselm's Ontological Argument ('I think it shows that either God exists or He is impossible; and if He was possible, then God would exist'), and by the reasonableness of the universe, and by the demands of morality. As for those physicists who believe the universe is a free lunch:

> I can only say I am quite certain they are wrong. There are no principles which are self-explanatory. If they say they would like to find one, I'll say Exactly so. God is defined not as the Old Man in the clouds, but as the self-explanatory principle which does explain the structure of the universe.

And yet Keith Ward had a sense of encountering a reality which was basically *personal*. What on earth could he mean by that?

> A sense of response. I must stress this is not because of any messages coming down the telephone line, but that your

life is in response to something – you are not just coming up against inert, meaningless, feelingless chairs and tables. There is something there which you are in constant response to and dependence upon.

While Michael Goulder is an atheist who used to be a believer, Keith Ward is the diametrical opposite: 'I was converted in a terribly traditional Christian way – that's not quite reputable for a philosopher. It was a sense of moral challenge. I can only say I took the gamble and I believe my experience verified the claim that there was a more valuable reality to which one could respond. It was a very evangelical experience.'

It will not surprise the reader who has got this far to be told that leaping into the evangelical experience is not for the present author. Perhaps I have too big a head and too small a heart – what C. S. Lewis called 'incurable intellectualism'; perhaps thirty years with the BBC programmed me to look always for both sides of the case; perhaps it is just too uninteresting. In any case I find myself much more at home with theologians like Rowan Williams, of Christ's College, Cambridge, who admits to having doubts daily about his faith: 'It seems to me an endemic part of trying to make sense.' This need to *make sense* is one of two key elements in Dr Williams's theology. The other, in a quotation from the French philosopher Simone Weil, is that 'God is the name we give to the connections we can't make'. By this he does not mean mere hypotheses that make it easier for people to understand things, but something like a sense of unity 'which would not ever be completely exhausted by description'. Struggling to keep his cat from taking over the microphone, Rowan Williams went on:

> It would be a very odd kind of human life that was based on the assumption that making sense was a waste of time. One of the things we characteristically do is to make sense. We look for patterns and regularities, we make things, build buildings, paint pictures, write poems – we make sense, we make stories and images of our own lives. We have a choice between saying either 'That depends entirely on my efforts and creativity', or it's a making sense which is also an exploration for more than just me;

something which feels the texture of things to see if a pattern suggests or even imposes itself.

It was at this point that I asked Dr Williams about doubt; because the question constantly presents itself to me – and it is fundamental to this whole case for or against God – *does* it make sense? Why should it make sense? What does making sense mean anyway? Dumping the cat, Rowan Williams resumed:

> Looking back over experience as a whole, and relying on other people's experience as well, it seems a lot of the time that a consistency and pattern is there, just round the corner – something you can never quite lay hold of. It has constantly to live together with the sense that it may all be an elaborate wish-fulfilment. I have no means of checking here and now whether I am right or not. I have got to decide to do the next thing either in faith or not in faith. It's not just a once and for all commitment, it's a decision to look for sense in that way which means making certain choices, performing certain actions, not just holding certain ideas.
>
> And then there's the difficult job, day by day, of seeing if that is workable. So there's no all-embracing solution to doubt, and I think it's a very important component of the religious enterprise; in that it makes you rightly suspicious of yourself, suspicious of your need to be consoled or cuddled by a cosmic friend. God's not necessarily consoling. The love of God is not a warm and cosy business very often, and you need always to be on the watch for that sort of wish-fulfilment. So insofar as doubt makes you aware of your capacity for self-deception, for coddling yourself, making it easy, then that negative moment is essential within faith.

Dr Williams had spoken of 'relying on other people's experience as well', and it came back to me once more that if there was a God perhaps one was more likely to discover Him by trusting people who trusted God, rather than by any process of argument. Yes, said Dr Williams, and that was exactly what was meant by the Communion of Saints: we were always having to talk about God obliquely, at an angle, by looking at the effects of belief:

> I could only say, hang around with representatives of one or another religious tradition – share the experiences of worship, entertain the images, the stories they tell. Look at the lives they point to as important lives, important saints, figures in their tradition: because I think it is profoundly true that the religious apprehension is caught, not taught.
>
> Never mind the word God for the moment, I think sometimes one has to put brackets round it in order to get people to recognise what that sense of love, trust and openness to reality amounts to. After all, T. S. Eliot, writing the *Four Quartets* – probably the most formidable religious poem of the century – uses the word God only twice. He wants, I think, to suggest there's a way of looking at the world which is deeply religious and which God does indeed cover and include eventually. But in order to feel that experience now in its fullness, you may need to put the word in brackets for a while.

5

Artists in Evidence

If the best way of talking about God is not to mention Him, perhaps we should steer clear of the sort of company we have been keeping in the past two or three chapters and follow the clue given us in the name of T. S. Eliot. For a great many people (especially the more highly educated) will tell you that they feel closest to God when they are experiencing the arts, and that they actually apprehend something of His nature in reading a poem, gazing at a painting, listening to Beethoven or Bach.

I have written elsewhere about the drawbacks of this. What about people who can't understand poetry and actively dislike Bach? Does God snobbishly reserve Himself for those of cultivated tastes, or is He to be found also in the tinklings of Victor Sylvester and the jingles of Noel Coward (where indeed Father Harry Williams *has* found Him)? And may there not be a confusion here between religious experience and aesthetic experience, between the divine and the beautiful; for although there may be a link between them – God the supremely powerful, the supremely good must also be the supremely beautiful – it is surely going too far to say that beautiful music *is* God, or even the word of God. Almost everyone who says they find God in the arts, and many who do not, say they also find Him in nature, particularly in landscape, and though there may be an even stronger case for claiming nature as the work of God, there are still differences of taste and the suspicion that we are in the realm of aesthetics.

Most of my atheist witnesses would insist that they enjoyed the arts quite as much as my believers. Sir Alfred Ayer says he is 'very fond of literature, very fond of painting, even fond of professional football – watching Tottenham Hotspur probably lose this evening'; and my Indian atheist, P. C. Chatterji, related an extraordinary experience of nature which any believer would have taken as an experience of God:

It was funny. I've always found the mountains have a strange effect on me, and it was up in a lovely little place now on the border between India and Pakistan – a little valley with lovely birch trees and the blue, blue water of the Kishengunga River. One of the mountains is just solid rock, and the sun used to play on that and produce wonderful colours. I was sitting there early one morning, watching all this with the sun coming up; and then suddenly I found I was laughing – I was rolling about on the ground laughing. Well, that was it.

And you will remember that Chatterji is also deeply affected by mystical poetry. But it does not seem to him that this need be anything to do with God. Marghanita Laski has made a study of ecstatic experiences and she, too, has chosen to reject the explanation that they are encounters with the All Powerful. But that does not mean that, when she steps out of her cottage on Hampstead Heath on a fine Spring morning she does not feel any sort of a twinge:

People have described it very often. It's the kind of experience you get from art, from nature, from religion, from sport, from childbirth, from love of your children, from Christian charity – no matter what. It's one of the (I should have thought) slightly pathological events that happens to human beings; but that it's immensely valuable in that you emerge from it with your brain in a better state than before. I don't think it's neurotic; but every writer, every artist knows how to use it.
For instance if – to use Henry James's phrase – you put the material you think you're going to need into the deep world of the unconscious and let it macerate there, one way of getting it out is to put a good record on the gramophone, go for a walk on Hampstead Heath, something of that kind. Then comes the ecstatic experience, greater or smaller, and probably something comes out that you didn't expect. Coleridge did this, you know: he

collected the material for a great epic on The Seasons, and what came out was The Ancient Mariner.

This seems to me very like what happens in the deepest kind of prayer: what *may* come out is the will of God, or one of Frances Young's loud thoughts. One can choose – *as we always must be able to* – to interpret these experiences otherwise, but, once again, if there is a God why should He not be at work in the subconscious, too? It does not follow from this that everything that emerges from that subconscious should be taken as of divine inspiration, any more than we can assume that our conscious mind is infallible: the Church has strict rules for the testing of private revelation. But if reason can 'point towards' the probability of God, then perhaps some of these 'slightly pathological events' can be taken as doing the same.

John Mortimer doubts it, though he is mildly interested in the artistic approach to faith:

That's another possibility: the Malcolm Muggeridge approach to God as the artist – that God is writing some huge transcendental *King Lear* and that we are having to play it. If you happen to be lined up to have your eyes gouged out, that's because it is a good curtain for Act I, or whatever it is. I could understand that, but I'm not sure I could forgive it . . .

I think that aesthetic experience is perhaps the nearest I could get to the idea of God. I can understand a mystic religion. I can understand moments when you feel at one with the universe, at one with nature, with the country-side. I don't believe that has any moral content, because I don't believe the great mystics behaved very well: all they did was sit and have those rather wonderful experiences – they didn't do anybody any particular good. But that I find acceptable.

One of the things I find incredibly difficult to understand is when you see the films of David Attenborough, when you see the incredible complication of the universe – did God go to all those enormous lengths to invent birds which were only able to eat by dropping snails onto hard rocks, miles up in the Andes? Or is that an accident? These are areas that I find very puzzling. And the awful things these tiny beasties do to one another! Almost as bad as the Mohammedans do to each other, too.

John Mortimer, as we all know, is a bit of a joker. Not so the novelist and philosopher Iris Murdoch, whose interview was probably the most intensely serious of all those I conducted. In one way and another, religion haunts all her books (as it seems to haunt her) and she finds herself unable to believe in God while at the same time unable to do without the sacraments. What seems to speak most deeply to her condition is the concept of holiness, both in things like the Eucharist and in people like the saints. But:

> I can't make sense for myself of the concept of the Christian God, or indeed of any God. Obviously one's not talking about chaps who live on Olympus or deities who have only local significance: one's talking of this universal, profound entity who is usually spoken of in our Judaeo-Christian world as a person – and I can't make sense of this. It isn't that I think the idea is empty – obviously it isn't empty, it is overfull, if anything – but it is not something that I can believe in.
>
> I was brought up as an Anglican and learnt to pray as soon as I could speak; and I took it for granted that I could speak to God. I knew all about the Trinity when I was about six years old. All this was absolutely deep in one's soul, and I think it still is in mine . . . But I feel the idea of personality is simply out of place. If one thinks of Good taking the place of God, one doesn't have conversations with Goodness. In fact the idea seems to me really rather a dangerous one. To take the idea of personality over that border seems to me to be almost wrong.

Miss Murdoch simply does not feel that there is anything urging or encouraging her or laying out a significant pattern before her: 'I think the basis of what confronts us is a kind of chaos.' She, like most of the non-believers I spoke to, is very concerned with the preservation of morality and would like to think that religion and morality were 'absolutely continuous with each other', as one might see in saintly people – 'and if you ever get near one, I think you're lucky and impressed and affected'. She likes the way religion gives this sort of holiness a larger emotional charge, connecting it up with some kind of mythology, which is one reason why she would regret the passing of picturesque religion and its eclipse by a religionless morality. The highest morality, she thinks, must have a religious vision. Irish Murdoch went on:

> I believe the essence of that vision would be some notion of a ground of being – not in the sense of a personal God, but the sense that the fundamental thing in human life is something to do with virtue and goodness; and that this is not just a special subject which some people want to adopt, but is everywhere; that the whole of your activities all day long are connected with this obligation or magnetism of a reality.
>
> I was thinking it would be terribly sad for the planet if the great religious symbols were to disappear. For instance, the most potent one in our society is the image of Christ . . . I can't banish Christ from my life. He's been in my life ever since I was a child. And this historical accident is also something which I treasure and would not want to be without. Now the question is, if one abandons Christian doctrine, in what sense can one keep the ritual and the great religious images, except as something frightfully personal and private?

Rather like my Jewish Humanist, Ze'ev Katz, Iris Murdoch would prefer to drop the word God but keep the word religion. Is one really possible without the other, though? Miss Murdoch looks hopefully to the radical theologians to make the Christian God rather less hard to swallow in one respect:

> I think it is worth noticing that a lot of Protestant theologians, in a quiet way, are telling us that we don't have to believe in the Incarnation; that we don't have to believe Christ is God, that's not essential. I am thinking of people like Don Cupitt and Maurice Wiles and a lot one could mention who in one way and another are suggesting the moves that we have got to make now. And of

course religion is always making moves – Christianity is a great series of terrific and often very intellectual moves.

The move we have got to make now is to realise that belief in the Incarnation is not essential: which leaves the place of Christ very strange – but perhaps (as it were) He could look after Himself. But then that moves the question over to what we mean by God.

Well, here one wonders whether some kind of theological-philosophical doctrine which could be brought to everybody is in the process of emerging; or whether it is too late, whether the whole thing is collapsing, whether there won't be churches, there won't be Christianity as we know it a century from now: which I should be very sorry to think, because I would be very much on the side of theologians hurrying to rescue the future of this whole mode of thinking.

But to most Christians, their faith is not – or not just – a mode of thinking. It is a way of seeing, hearing, feeling and responding. And while it is true that there have been substantial intellectual shifts in Christian doctrine over the centuries, and that the most considerable one taking place now concerns the Incarnation, I very much doubt whether Dean Cupitt, Professor Wiles and the *Myth* group will, or should, persuade believers that what they are feeling and responding to is a fundamental ground of virtue and goodness. If you read or listen to saintly people, you find them saying that faith is not just about goodness and virtue but also about many other things which are much less humanistic and utilitarian: a sense of direction, a sense of meaning (though Miss Murdoch does not discern this), a sense also of wonder, love and praise, and of the divinity of Christ. I am somewhat towards the *Myth* side myself in saying 'If Jesus was not God, He is now'; but I think there is far too much in the Incarnation that is meaningful, useful and true for us to abandon it altogether and say that Jesus is 'just a very good man'.

Miss Murdoch's hankering after Him is moving; but I think Christians would say that she has an incomplete, unconvinced image of Him when she says:

The Cross worries me, because Christ doesn't die. He survives and goes to Heaven and sits on the right hand of God. And this doesn't happen as far as I can see to human beings. Human beings die and suffer without any reward and without their suffering doing anybody any good either. I think there is a sort of terribleness in human fate. I think one sees this since Hitler even more than in the past. I think there is something terrible about the planet . . . that in a way you have got to realise the ineffectiveness of goodness and of suffering.

Perhaps because she *is* a philosopher as well as a novelist, Iris Murdoch presents us with a bleak outlook: a universe of cruelty and chaos without purpose, where goodness and suffering are largely ineffectual, and where the only hope for religion is to make a god of that same ineffectual goodness. But that is not how all artists see it; indeed it is striking how few poets, painters and musicians have been non-believers.

P. J. Kavanagh, the poet, has been a Roman Catholic from the cradle. He stopped practising for some years and told himself he had been brainwashed, but in the end was unable *not* to believe. 'It was fruitful – I've always found it worked. I do actually believe there is an educative process going on. I do not believe with Dylan Thomas that one should rage against it. A grace-filled resignation can be arrived at. I am *content* to believe.' But, I argued, the sort of experience that Thomas was raging against – undeserved pain and humiliation – was a pretty drastic way of educating people, surely?

I don't see what we have deserved. I do find people complain an enormous amount. I cannot see why so many people think things should be better than they are. I don't see where their idea of what is better, what is ideal, comes from. It seems to me we get *more* than we deserve. If one is in any sort of good state . . . the pleasures of creation, of society, of sensation surround us and are there to be enjoyed. There is a glory and a mystery and excitement all round us, which many people who complain a lot, refuse to look at, refuse to accept, refuse to take in. It's all there, like a great box of sweets, and they say 'No, these aren't the sweets we wanted.'

But what if one was not in 'a good state'? With permission, I hit below the belt by reminding Kavanagh that his first wife had died young and died in agony – had she deserved that?

> I think the whole question of desert seems to me perfectly extraordinary. The short answer is No. But what do we mean by deserve? I don't see where it comes into it. Of course, I was by no means as cool about it then; but I'll tell you something else. When that happened, within moments, I had an experience. I wouldn't dream of calling it a mystical experience, but a huge influx of joy.
>
> *GP*: Joy?
>
> *Kavanagh*: Joy, yes. And noise. These are all images, and it took a spatial form – it did seem like great rays coming down from above, and the world felt filled with consolation, like a tank up to the brim – every sort of balm and consolation and joy one could imagine. The dark tunnel was there to go down afterwards; but then to reduce such an experience and say it was Hyperaesthesia would seem to me extraordinarily disloyal to what seemed to me as real as anything that's ever happened to me.

And it would be disloyal to my own memory to deny that those last two passages were as impressive as anything I heard on this enquiry. Mr Kavanagh struck me as being a pretty tough character and far from mystical or even particularly aesthetic:

> I am not sure that artists are aesthetic people at all. I don't think that is the prime thing. It is almost like a form of intense concentration, which involves a process of illumination, of connections, of lightning gaps, of the movement of a current of electricity between apparently disparate things: and for a moment you see that they are connected and you feel, yes, you can make a shape out of this, you can really do something with this and express it. Usually it falls apart in your hands; but it is this lightning flash – you know, Michelangelo's finger of God stretched out to Adam, and the fingers don't touch.
>
> But it's not only that, it's connections: and once you have ever had the experience of the connectedness of

apparently wildly disparate things, you are never quite the same again. The poem or the picture may fall apart in your hands, but you feel there might well be a connectiveness in the world.

Freud, I hazarded, would probably conclude that P. J. Kavanagh was neurotic:

I don't know enough about Freud really to go on about him. But I do think one has to be very careful not to erect reason into the be-all and end-all and put it firmly on the throne. Reason is extremely important and anyone who thinks it isn't is an idiot. But there are aspects of life which reason can't quite cope with – which does not make them unreasonable. They have to be dealt with in another way. Intuition – goodness knows – can be a lazy word; but it can be a very real power.

I do not suppose the positivists would be happy about this resort to intuition. But I could not help recalling that, for at least the fifth time in the enquiry, a witness had described something quite extraordinary to me and then insisted that it was as *real* to him or her as anything that had ever happened; and they had all been statements of a sort to put at stake the integrity, even the whole personality, of the witness.

I was perhaps on less sure ground with John Tavener, the composer. Not that he is unreliable, but as a devout Russian Orthodox he inhabits the world of mysticism as a daily routine, and in any case would rather play his music (which is profoundly religious) than try to put his beliefs into words. He is intuitive to the core ('My rational mind never answers musical problems') and the deep part of him has never doubted the existence of God. His personal revelations made some of the others' sound rather insubstantial:

I don't normally talk about these sort of things – the almost visionary things that have happened in my life – but I had a waking dream (I was actually awake) and I heard a voice in the room and the voice said to me, 'You are Simon of Cyrene and you will carry my cross'. Now I don't believe

that this was the voice of Christ; but I believe that it was
something telling me, almost encouraging me, to go on.

I suppose I have come to realise what might be the cross
that I have to carry: to bring what I love of Byzantium, of
Orthodoxy, to England; and although I am not fanatical
about ecumenism, perhaps I can do more through music
than through endless discussions. I was asked at the
beginning of this year to set the All Night Vigil Service,
let's say three hours of music which has to be prayed to,
and I feel that is my cross because I feel very lonely in this
task.

Tavener is very far from believing that all great music speaks
of God, even if it claims to be religious music. To him Bach,
Beethoven, Monteverdi, indeed most western music, does not
'let God through'. Some of it seems to him actively demonic;
and John Tavener is personally acquainted with Satan:

I think maybe people have forgotten the horror . . . I have
once seen what I thought was the Incarnate Devil when I
was composing my opera *Therese*; and I found myself
crouching below my window-sill because I thought the
Devil was trying to come in. I think at the time I was so
completely terrified, it was as much as I could do to
scramble back into bed. I think the Devil not only can
affect people's actions and people's lives, but it can also
affect art. I will be very unpopular for saying this, but I
think masterpieces can be created that are evil or Devil-
inspired. I would throw Berg's *Lulu* out of the window –
masterpiece though it may be musically and technically. I
don't give a damn – it is a work of evil.

Like the icon-painters of Byzantium, Tavener regards
prayer, the sacraments and fasting as essential to the process of
composition. But fasting, I suggested, could affect the chemis-
try of the body: was there not a danger that he was distorting his
own mentality?

Yes, I think there is a danger and I am certain I have fallen
victim to this, but there is a paradox. I relate to people in a
much deeper way while I am fasting and composing. I
don't think that can be a distortion if I am relating more

warmly, more lovingly, more openly as the weight is
dropping off me physically. I am aware of what you say,
but if one is loving and more transparent, it must be a good
thing.

John Tavener also spoke of 'receiving gifts from people who
had died' and I realized that he meant something far more
mysterious than cash legacies:

In my case it has been almost exclusively the gift of music.
A neighbour of mine who lived over the road died very
suddenly, and his wife came over and asked me if I would
come. And I prayed by his body, and came back, and
recollected myself; and very soon after – suddenly, it
seemed to come from nowhere – a piece of music was fully
born in me. I sat down and wrote it, just like that, and it
contained only one word – I don't know why, I hadn't
been thinking of it – it was the Greek word for glory: *Doxa*.
It lasts about ten minutes but it was a very strange
experience because it appeared to have been a gift from
this man. I remember Father Malachi Lynch – a Roman
Catholic Carmelite monk – again, after I'd prayed by his
body, I felt, minutes after, notes were already coming into
my head and I felt again the gift he had given me was to
write a requiem for him. This has happened almost every
time anybody close to me has died, but not in quite such a
dramatic way as the first example I gave.

One can well understand how an artist like this is totally
unimpressed by the argument that science has explained away
all the empty gaps in our understanding that God used to fill:

Because I think finally one has to go *beyond* everything.
One has to go beyond art, go beyond nature, till one is
living literally with the Desert Fathers. It is very difficult
to be living as a Desert Father in this century, but with
one's eyes closed. Even as an Orthodox I can say there
must be a time when one can go beyond the Icon, go
beyond all nature, go beyond everything in this world and
just have one's eyes shut.

So John Tavener knows of a state in which there is no more
argument, no more experience even, but simply a kind of

absorbed *being* – out of which a voice may call upon him to take up his cross, or the Devil Incarnate may lurk at his window.

I think Jonathan Miller, Doctor of Medicine, would have diagnosed this as verging on the schizophrenic; but in general Miller – who simply lacks the faculty of belief – is not inclined to analyze faith as a tangle of psychiatric conditions. Being deeply involved in the arts, he can no more dismiss religious experiences as mere brain-events than he can dismiss, say, a painting by Vermeer as a mere arrangement of chemicals: 'They are not just brain-events, they are also events in the mind, in the imagination, and to dismiss them merely as that is, I think, to miss the point.'

Jonathan Miller is yet another of those fascinating cases who cannot leave religious images alone and yet cannot deduce from them what the believer does. He is grateful for the fact that he lives in a society in which belief has played so strong a part, because he believes that it creates all sorts of emblems, structures, narratives and images without which life would be extremely dry and impoverished. He admits that, in a sense, he is taking a free ride and not paying his fare: no wonder he is fearful of saying things which might bring a posse of vicars to his doorstep, claiming him for their own:

> I return to the Bible a great deal now in a way that I didn't when I was fifteen years younger; not for solace, not because I believe, but because there are certain energies in those stories – certainly no comforts, particularly. I go now every year to hear the *Matthew Passion*, not simply because I like Bach but because I follow the words very closely as the music unfolds. And it gives me a sense of vigour and strength to have gone through the narrative account of that passion whose transcendental significance has no meaning for me at all, and yet I find the constant reiteration, year by year, of St Peter's denial, of his tears, of the road to Golgotha, of the Crucifixion, of the moment of death, of the interment – they are ritual necessities to me without, in fact, having a smidgen of belief in any of it.
>
> I am moved by the spectacle of people moved by religion . . . I can remember the only time that I have ever been

moved to tears by something which was not a direct
emotional incident in my own life. Five or six years ago I
was walking with my wife up the aisle of St Anthony's
Cathedral in Padua, about lunchtime. And I was passing
by one of the side chapels, and there was a man in a
raincoat, his hand still gripping his briefcase; he was
kneeling at the altar steps receiving the sacrament; and the
spectacle of this man reaching forward, his tongue poked
out, with his hand still gripping his briefcase (representing
his day which had been briefly set aside, and which was to
be resumed a few moments later) taking his soul seriously
– it moved me, and it moves me now to think of it.

GP: So what's it all about – or is it just absurd?

Miller: Well, I don't think it's absurd. I do think there is
something very peculiar about us as a species, while I do
believe that we are in fact an accident, and we're put
together randomly; I don't think we are the realisation of
some purpose. I don't think we are on the summit of some
scale of being which is going to (as it were) act out some
redemptive drama for God's entertainment or satisfaction.
I nevertheless find myself deeply moved by the thought
that this concatenation of stuff that has got together *is*
movable in this way, even to a sinful disbeliever like
myself. I find myself startled by the experience I've just
described.

Now I can't argue from that to a state of belief; and some
people – carnivorous, evangelical Christians – leap out
from the vestry and say 'Ha-ha! This is it! That is belief,
dear boy!' and try to usher me into the church. But it's *not*
belief – it simply leaves me with the sense of being moved.

The intriguing thing here is that Jonathan Miller has had –
and who knows? perhaps been sent – enough religious experience to support belief *if he chose it*. But he does not, and I am
sure we must respect that and even be grateful for it; for I think
that if there is a God belief in Him must be slightly precarious
and always challenged by intelligent and conscientious disbe-
lievers like Miller. It would be trivializing to explain away his
resistance to belief in psychoanalytical terms, though I reckon
that could be done; more obvious, in his earlier testimony, is the

revulsion he feels from the traditional images of the Church's God as the Wosbee commandant, the setter of impossible tasks, the tormentor of mankind. If there is a God, I suspect He is not like that at all.

Anyhow, it had been a stimulating session with Jonathan Miller and we clattered away happily over the loose tiles in his entry hall to pack up our recording gear in the converted ice-cream van outside. It was shortly afterwards that we found ourselves with Ronald Eyre, another man of the arts, but who had reached very different conclusions from his experience. Not that Eyre was any more enchanted with the Old Testament God than Miller was:

> I'm amazed when sometimes I switch on the radio in the afternoons and hear extremely elegant cut-glass voices singing evensong from one of our cathedrals, but actually talking about bloody Jewish adventures. Nothing I could tell you in the form of a dream could be more bizarre, I think, than the survival of that tribal history in our rinsed western circumstances. I find that freaky. Listening to a creed, for instance, you hear people use the word 'believe'. But I hear a creed as a form of battle-cry, appropriate to some time when the threat of the opposite was there, and you had to have a creed as if the sea was coming in at the back door and you had to block it. But when the sea retreats, protecting a place where there is no threat seems to me to be a waste of time. I don't mean scrub the creeds, but I do mean that for me they seem like relics of crisis . . . I remember we had a Bishop Christopher Butler who advised us on some of the films we made; and one of the producers was a bit anxious about my inability to handle the word *believe* as 'to take on something which you have no right to think from any other source, so you have to make a jump and *believe*'. And Bishop Butler said, 'Well, I believe in a creed to the extent that it's true'. Now that, of course, I will go along with totally. I will not believe in a creed to the extent that somebody else suggests I should.

The belief of a free spirit, which Ronald Eyre undoubtedly is; although this will disturb many traditional believers who rather oddly maintain that belief is not belief unless we are all believing the same thing; which is not only impossible but simply does not happen. The pretence that it can and should leads to the fiction that there is an unchanging view of God – the Christian Faith – that was set out in the Bible and can easily be restored by pruning away the later heresies and developments. There is no such basic faith, and probably was not from the moment Jesus died. But the insistence that there must be powerfully deters those who would like to appropriate the divine to themselves, but on their own terms.

Ronald Eyre's sense of whatever-it-is-we-are-talking-about is no longer attached to the figure of Christ, though once it was:

I mean there is a certain soft Christ I used to be very attentive to, somebody who almost justified the limpness of my own approach to lots of things. I happen to think now it is perfectly proper to be pretty agressive some-times, to be firm. The ego-lessness talked about some-times by a certain kind of Buddhist is something I think is very dangerous. A Jew will tell you it is part of your human responsibility to stake out your territory and occupy it. But the sort of 'wet' Christ that justified a lot of the limpness in my family is one that I am glad to see go to the wall.

I certainly do have, from some source, a notion that whatever happens I am supported. I don't mean that my whims are supported and that if I decided to terminate my life that would not break the pattern; but I just have, underneath, a notion of being part of some intention. Not all of me is alive, but there is some sort of organic, quiet shifting, moving, or the possibility of it going on, and I must attend to that. God is somewhere in that area for me . . .

And if you were to ask how I would characterise God, I would associate Him with joy; and I would also associate Him with a certain lightness of touch – playfulness – because the opposite of that, downwardness and over-seriousness, are almost my personal devils.

And a God who is sensed as overwhelmingly a God of joy is a very personal God, too. It is hardly the main impression to be drawn from the Bible. But Ronald Eyre seems to get his revelations – his loud thoughts – in the form of dreams, 'crystalizations of things which I can't be too grateful for. Very mysterious, usually at very critical moments.' And he gave me a striking example:

> I had a very strong feeling of walking along a ridge, next to a green field, and I knew that I was going to die. That was quite simple. I was walking along this ridge and that was fine. I was curiously calm – not merry, but sort of all right – and this seemed to me quite proper, accepting what had to be. Down the slope of the hill was a little slide, as if from a children's playground, full of slippery talcum powder; with a very hairy Old English sheepdog trying to climb up it – sneezing, dust in its eyes, doing exactly the wrong thing.
>
> Well, I recognised my friend the sheepdog absolutely: an accurate image of the way I live a lot of my life, trying to get up a talcy slide the wrong way. Why don't I just roll on the grass? Why do I go in for all this sort of nonsense? Now the hope for me in this is that a lot of the time I feel I am only the dog; but the dream tells me I am the dog *plus* the man walking along the high ridge. Does that make sense?
>
> *GP*: In a splendid surrealist way it does.
>
> *Eyre*: But it's got to be surrealist, you see. That's why a lot of religious formulations to me fall short. They are not quite bizarre enough to fit the bizarreness of being alive.

And we wondered together whether this was not one of the mistakes that modern theology made in struggling with modern atheism: that it tried to play the same game on the same rational level, instead of jumping off the ground, flapping its wings and flying – that it was not joyous and surrealist enough.

Detachment from literal, logical truth is one of the great advantages of the arts as expressions of faith. A poem does not have to be possible, a painting of the Holy Trinity is not pretending to be a photographic likeness, and a piece of music cannot be translated into words at all. And yet when people set out to formulate their love and admiration of God they use all these media with the passionate conviction that they are expressing something important and real. Some would say they are mercifully liberated from reality altogether, but to the artist the liberation is from pettifogging correspondences which otherwise keep him or her earthbound and inarticulate.

Certainly if I wanted to convey what it feels like to apprehend God, I would have to cite a painting like El Greco's *Burial of Count Orgaz*, with its rising tiers of dignitaries and angels; or a piece of music like Sibelius's eery song *Pa Verandan Vid Havet*: or George Herbert's dazzling sonnet on *Prayer*:

> Prayer, the Church's banquet, Angels' age,
> God's breath in man returning to his birth,
> The soul in paraphrase, heart in pilgrimage,
> The Christian plummet, sounding heaven and earth;
> Engine against the Almighty, sinner's tower,
> Reverséd thunder, Christ-side-piercing spear,
> The six-days' world transposing in an hour,
> A kind of tune, which all things hear and fear;
> Softness and peace, and joy, and love, and bliss,
> Exalted manna, gladness of the best,
> Heaven in ordinary, man well drest,
> The milky way, the bird of Paradise,
> Church-bells beyond the stars heard, the soul's blood,
> The land of spices, something understood.

Those last two lines, with their straining of the ears, dilating of the nostrils, stirring of the mind, capture for me exactly the growing suspicion that there is, after all, 'something there', and that if it is to be understood it is not to be in terms of philosophical propositions.

There are, alas, very few in the Church today who have the kind of leaping imagination that Herbert displays. One of the few (perhaps because he is also a considerable poet in his own right) is John Vernon Taylor, the Bishop of Winchester, whose embarrassment I shall not spare in calling him also one of the few unquestionably holy people I have met. It is quite simply good to be with him and to hear him speaking in that low, vibrant voice.

The arts mean a lot to him, too, especially music: 'It isn't to be rationally explained in scientific terms – it isn't just a matter of vibrations reaching your diaphragm. You are in an area of knowledge which is not dissimilar to the knowing of God. I think the artists of whatever sort are striving after truth. They are the conveyors of the mystery, the beauty, the truth and therefore strong pointers towards the reality of things.'

And the reality of things to John V. Taylor is ultimately God. But what sort of a God does the poet-bishop believe in?

Gradually I have come to realise, what I certainly didn't realise as a young man – that when I am talking about God I am not talking about *a* anything. That is precisely the difference. He isn't *a* being, isn't even the Supreme Being. He is Being itself, from which all beings derive their existence. One might almost say God has dreamed everything. If for one moment He stopped dreaming, it would all stop. There would not be – there would never have been – anything. And so He is this inexhaustible source of the very power of existing: being, rather than a being.

GP: Then how can He be at all personal?

Taylor: You really do feel sometimes you are on the edge of an abyss, because you cannot imagine what it is like to be Being Itself. Nonetheless, the sense of this source of all being as personal – being able to become the source from which one feels one is addressed or called – seems to be almost fundamental to the experience of religious people. Though to be honest I think the Buddhists would deny that sense of a personal or of a God who addresses them in any way.

GP: Has your faith ever been badly shaken?

Taylor: There are times when I wonder whether I have just been kidding myself; times when I am afraid of death and think 'Well, perhaps at the last moment I shall suddenly realise I have been fooling myself all along. And watching the suffering of somebody else, that does make it difficult.'

GP: How can you come to terms with totally undeserved suffering, under the rule of a good God?

Taylor: I think you have to come to a deeper understanding of what you mean by 'the rule'. I myself have moved to the position where I no longer think of God as a super chess-player who, if only He will, can move any of the pieces around and win the game; nor even of a God who, if only we prayed hard enough, or if only He was willing, would come and intervene and take away the suffering.

I think that God is engaged in a much longer and more dangerous adventure, in which there is a great deal of accident around: that's the sort of world that God has made and allowed and has submitted Himself to. I think He intervenes through that part of the universe that is capable of being open to Him, namely ourselves . . . But I don't believe in a God who can suddenly raise up a storm or make the sun stand still or take away something that is there threatening.

At this I could imagine loud cries of complaint from atheists insisting that this was precisely the God in which Christians were supposed to believe, and had believed for centuries. I knew from past conversations that Bishop Taylor would assert that the Church had been plain wrong about that, or had taken far too long to realise the truth about it. But if there could be no miraculous interventions, what about the miracles of Jesus? Another shock:

I think they were the miracles of a man. I think that everything Jesus did, He did in His humanity. He showed the full length of what a man might be capable of if he was completely open to God . . . I believe Jesus was God – I don't hesitate to say that – but I believe He was God completely contained in His manhood. There are no bits of Him that you can say Ah! that wasn't the man, that was the God working . . . You asked me earlier whether I have had times when I really did doubt God. Well, there have been several times when the only reason I went on believing in God was because *He* did. And I would rather go down into the dark, as a fool, with Him than find any other sort of God.

The Bishop thinks that serious atheism deserves to be taken seriously, and admits that he has met people who held the atheist position deeply and totally 'but whose integrity in holding it struck me as something very near sanctity'. What linked such people to God (whether they acknowledged it or not) was their love of truth and their openness. 'The good atheist is never, I think, one hundred per cent certain, and usually admits it . . . And very often their atheism is the fruit of their caring for humanity.' There were, he added, plenty of *bad* reasons for believing in God.

But what if, in the end, the unbeliever decided to take the plunge, how did he go about it?

Chesterton said the worst moment in the life of an atheist was when his heart was overflowing with thankfulness and he had no one to thank. So sometimes gratitude alone may make one feel it would be good to explore this, begin to take it seriously, to see what happens . . . Then I've talked about the call, the sense that somehow there is a Thou in all this universe, it isn't just an it, and I feel myself *addressed*. It is as if one were given the end of a golden string – a clue – and then it is up to you to decide whether it is worth following up. It may lead nowhere. But on the other hand, it has a sense of value, a sense of ultimate importance: it's worth following to see what you find.

6

The Scene of the Crime

One of the weaknesses of religion is that it sets the scene for its own fulfilment. It erects special buildings specially furnished, it composes special music and liturgies conducted by specialists in special vestments on special days of the week. Everything is calculated to heighten consciousness and arouse sympathetic vibrations. Even if nothing is visible, surely it cannot all be about nothing? A religion like Christianity is so ancient and elaborate that it confirms itself through an elegant network of cross-references, supported by a noble army of saints, martyrs and institutions which one can hardly dismiss without de-molishing the integrity of an entire civilization. A seeker like myself, who cannot help picking at the structure, is indignantly challenged, 'Do you mean to say the gospels are lying?', to which I can only reply that I think they are trying to tell the truth as the authors saw it, in the terms that came naturally to them; but that neither is quite adequate to my understanding today. But such an answer does leave me feeling guilty for my impudence.

The philosopher Wittgenstein (in whose bleak bedroom in Cambridge I once spent the night) seems to have become increasingly intrigued by religion; but he regarded religious belief as a kind of game on its own, not to be tampered with by science or logical positivism. To him it could not be based upon evidence, like science – indeed, Wittgenstein thought real hard evidence would spoil everything – but was only to be assessed by the difference belief made to the life of the believer. It was simply not accessible to the categories of logic, and Wittgen-stein thought none the worse of it for that.

So we are still left asking 'But is it true? Is there really something out-there-and-in-here, of which religion tries to construct some kind of model to which we can then respond and which will respond to us? Or is it just a beautiful wish-fulfilling word-game, perhaps healthy (or perhaps not) but in the end an illusion?'

As we have seen, there are philosophers and scientists who do not agree that God is wholly inaccessible to their disciplines. Even so, they do not claim that they can prove His existence with finality: only that they can point towards a high probability that He exists. Some of the artists we met in the previous chapter are doing the same thing from another direction, that of intuition and apprehension, though they are often applying a deliberately heightened sensitivity. What I want to do now is to bring matters back to the scene of the crime, the everyday world in which people work and suffer, live and die mostly without the benefit of holy words and music or even of loud thoughts and electrifying presences. I want to see how God, or the idea of Him, works in practice rather than theory. For, surely, if there is a God, knowledge of Him must make some difference; and if there is a difference for the believer, this will at least be one more bundle of pointers towards that probability.

We shall have to deal seriously with the problem of evil; though I must not overlook one comment of Don Cupitt's which seems to play into the hands of the atheists:

> Many people begin with a cosy religious theory of the world, and then they find the facts of life tell against it. They have been working the wrong way round. It is *because* the world and our own natures are so unsatisfactory that we need religion. So on my account, evil does not falsify faith: it makes faith necessary. For me religion *starts* from the fact of evil; it is a practical activity and it is meant for us to survive, to overcome evil, to give meaning and worth to life in the face of evil.
>
> So my faith starts from a realistic assessment of the human situation, and I move on from there. I think it is only people with a superstitious notion of religion who see evil as threatening to it. They have got it the wrong way round.

Religion, then, challenges evil – not the reverse. But Don Cupitt does not imagine a God who pursues Satan with a flaming sword; nor does he entertain what he would regard as the superstitious idea of God's universe being fundamentally on our side. 'It is up to us', he says, 'to affirm human dignity in the face of an indifferent universe.' It is noble, but it sounds like whistling in the dark. And the real objection to it is not that it is comfortless but that it is not what the most impressive believers know.

There are few people in my acquaintance who know more about the darkness than Margaret Bowker, historian, and wife of Professor John Bowker of Lancaster. The spiritual interplay between the two of them, since I first met them four years ago, has been moving to watch. For while Margaret, though a scholar, has always spoken of faith in feminine, maternal, intuitive terms, John has become progressively less 'scientific' in his religious talk and more of a poet. The reason is that Mrs Bowker has been going through a series of horrific operations for cancer (as she says, they have removed about everything they can remove), and they have both had to come to terms with the problem of suffering in a way that is very far from academic. Margaret, in particular, has a very strong case against God for choosing such a drastic way of telling her to slow down:

> I hate the pain. I hate having to wear prostheses and things like that. I hate the fact that I'm all the time looking to see if anybody has noticed. I hate the fact that the men look at you and think 'Oh, golly, she's going to throw hysterics on me because we don't really understand women in this situation.' And I hate the fact that somebody close to me – not my husband – said to me as I came out of the operation (prior to the radio-therapy, which is much worse) 'You're only half a woman'. I hate all this. But when I put my case, with tears and banging on the floor to God, I hear it coming back, 'You prayed that you would give yourself utterly to Me, how else could I have you?'

Margaret Bowker is thinking here of her former pride in academic achievement, of her workaholic addiction, and of her final breakthrough to 'feeling the resurrection', something she had been unable to do because 'my case against God was so great I couldn't even stop to listen'. But surely, I asked her, as a believer, the message of the Cross had been before her all the time?

I reckoned that the message of the Cross had got through and that God owed me an easy run. Well, He doesn't owe any of us anything, and that was my arrogance. It is no good my saying to Him, 'Lord, because you've done this to me, You owe me some special treats, some special experiences in prayer, some special warm feeling.' I know He doesn't owe me anything.

GP: But can you really blame God for the suffering you have been pitched into?

Margaret Bowker: This is a perpetual dialogue between myself and my husband. My husband keeps telling me that there could be a universe on no other terms, and that this means death – 'Unless the seed falls to the ground we cannot have the blooming of the plant. Unless you and I die there will be standing-room only, and shortly not even that, on this planet.'

I take this in a kind of way. But I still say now to God, 'If you really are God, you could have devised a planet on other terms.' My husband says that's impossible; but he's my husband, he's mortal.

I believe that to an Almighty God there are other possible terms of existence. Indeed, I think as we discover even more we are beginning to see that other forms of life are going to be possible on other planets which, perhaps, won't have all these constraints of suffering and death written into them. But the fact remains, I am born on this one, and if I kick against it I will never make anything of it. If I go on denying the terms on which this planet can exist, I am really saying I want this planet *not* to exist.

GP: Take it away and bring me a new one?

Bowker: Well, yes, that's what I would like to say to God: 'Bring me one where I don't see the children dying of leukemia. Take me away where I don't see the terrible TV shots of Ethiopia or West Africa. Take me away from El

Salvador. Take me away – or Stop the world, I want to get off!'

But nobody's going to stop the world; and that is why I have learned with age not to ask for what isn't built into the system. I do keep asking for a new creation, but I know that's cloud cuckoo land, and that in this creation what I must ask for is time to pray for all those who are undergoing suffering. So I say, 'All right, God, if you have to do something yet more catastrophic to me – well, we've agreed there aren't any other terms'. And insofar as I can say that, then the prayer for the others becomes easier; and I suspect that is why He has given me my freedom on such tough terms.

When anybody comes to me now to talk about anything, I know not to talk but to listen. That means they will pour out a great deal, and then it's up to me to discern what it is that God is trying to do with them. That's a very presumptuous statement. But I suggest to somebody in deep distress that they *pray* their grief – they say, 'God, you have done this to me, and it's hell and you don't seem to realise that I haven't got enough money, no resources, no relatives, but I've worshipped you all my life and you've not done it to anybody else in my road, but you've done it to me!' Well, let's hear that cry, let's stick out the listening and see what comes through. After a bit it is quite fantastic, the way a certain conviction begins to form in both of you. We stick with it, however awful it is. I've taken retreats where people have cried for eight days – and you must think I am the worst retreat-giver in Christendom. But if, through the tears they have learned trust, that is eight days well spent.

Whatever the future holds for Margaret Bowker, it is hard to believe that her life would have been of more value to others, or that she would have gone as deep into its meaning for herself, without her suffering. As her husband, John, put it:

There is no question that for those who quietly and patiently – often through great suffering – maintain their friendship with God, that that friendship transforms and changes the outcome in their lives and in the lives of others. The problem is, it's not like putting 5p in the slot and getting out a platform ticket. Yet everything is still to live for; and the help that God offers is so profound that, as it lays hold on one's life, there is no way you can possibly deny it or think one is simply deceiving oneself. It is in the consequence of belief that the reality of God begins not just to transform life but to transfigure it, in the direction of death understood as necessary end and as the means into life.

GP: But fundamentally, why do you believe in God?

John Bowker: Because He is.

GP: How do you know?

Bowker: Because of the transformation that occurs, not just painfully and slowly in my own case, but so manifestly in the lives of so many people that I have known. Something is transforming them; and that something seems to them to act within them and to act with them more like a personal relationship than in any other way. The question one has to ask is: given that profound transformation, what inference are we entitled to draw?

I am sure the sceptic would reply that we were not entitled to infer the existence of an independent God. He would agree that Margaret Bowker has courageously and magnificently made the best of a cruel fate by choosing to interpret it in a religious light; but might not a brave stoic have done as well? Indeed she might, and that would actually have been easier; for the stoic has only to endure the evil, she does not have to reconcile it with the existence of a good, loving and purposeful God. The fact that Margaret Bowker has done so suggests that she has extracted a much fuller meaning from her suffering and has found extensions from it that go far beyond the mere pathology of her condition: one would not have *expected* to find them. Nor is it that she has no alternative but to accept her suffering. She could, if she chose, simply rage against it – as she sometimes does. In spite of that she has come to see a purpose and fruitfulness behind the suffering, which comes at her in a form that *knows* her.

I think it is this sense of being known, personally, that

convinces many people of the reality of God. Exactly what it is that knows, it is impossible to describe by any other word. We probably could not discuss a wholly 'independent' God, just as we could not discuss the radiations from outer space without relying on the instruments that pick them up and show them to be there: our knowledge depends on their readings. But the believer is often aware of a slice or beam of consciousness which is exactly on his or her wavelength and which seems to *know* him or her in that way. Laying oneself open to such 'transmissions' is, I take it, what prayer is really about (and what Margaret Bowker and her retreatants were up to). The public God of the Church is an attempt to gather together, shape and organize countless millions of knowings and to make a response to them. But this would be impossible if they did not have sufficient features in common to convince believers they were all known by the same Knower.

For some people this mutual knowledge is simple and serene. Early in this investigation we met Jane Adams, who had lost her four-year-old son, and her relationship with God is a very direct one:

> I think the Lord makes me feel more complete. I feel loved by him, totally loved. What I learnt through losing Matthew is that anybody can just die at any time; or leave you – he won't necessarily be with you all the time, even though you may have come to expect it. But the Lord is with you always. He'll go through a heavy situation with you and He'll be there for all eternity. He'll never leave me and it's a joy to know that I'll never be alone . . . When Matthew died, He didn't just take him away and leave me stranded. He gave me two very close friends, one who lost her own little boy a few months later, so we've been able to share with each other; and another friend who would just listen and understand.

Gerry O'Collins, the professor at the Gregorian in Rome, says he finds God constantly intervening like this 'through the love and kindness of other human beings – an extraordinary experience of God's presence' and that it is often at times of tragedy that this presence is felt:

I would not want to say that I have suffered very much in my life; but two or three times people have let me down with unintentioned cruelty, and the strange thing about those situations is that I felt God there, and I began to appreciate the cry of abandonment of Jesus on the Cross. He was addressing the One who was silent and not doing anything. But He knew His God was there; and in my own very small way, through those experiences of suffering, I felt able to understand for the first time what that cry of abandonment was about, and how God could be mysteriously there in situations that were deeply desolate and savagely cruel.

It was the savagery and desolation of the Holocaust that started this Case against God. Bernard, the survivor I met in Israel, had had no sense of the Almighty watching over him in the camps, but he did experience the godliness in human protectors. In the circumstances it is marvellous that he has contrived any faith at all:

One of the worst things I remember was being with my Father – Mother had already disappeared by this time – when this ghetto in Krakow was being liquidated (that's the term they used). We ended up in this camp, and one morning there was a roll-call and they gathered all the children, and we just knew what was going to happen to us. We knew the killings that were going on out of our vision, with trucks coming daily with people who were just mowed down. My Father just looked at me with utter helplessness, and when we got to Auschwitz, he ended up going one way and I the other.

When we got out of the train it was just madness, we didn't know what was happening – dogs were loosed – we were being driven by prisoners and by the SS: formed into a line five abreast and then gradually narrowed down into a single line at the end; and there a prisoner went up to me and said in Polish 'Lie about your age – you're older than what you are', and then he disappeared. There were many miracles in which people assisted me. Being small, scrawny, starved, men would give a piece of bread, a piece of clothing, and when we were marching they put me in the middle where I was protected.

Somehow they saw their own survival coming through me in some way.

And so today, after years of trying to blot the experience from his memory, Bernard is trying to ensure that those who saved him did not sacrifice in vain. But what did God have to do with all this?

I don't think God had anything to do with it – absolutely nothing. I view God as an entity that allows us to create with His blessings whatever we choose. We have a free choice, a free will. So it's not as if we can blame God. I think it is Man who is on trial, though we superimpose God. From my point of view, nothing but good comes from God: no evil, no unrighteousness, no cruelty, no punishment. In my view, God says Yes to everything. The question is, what do we, as human beings, project onto Him, and say 'Oh, God told us to do this'.

Rabbi Hugo Gryn underwent very similar experiences in the camps, but his reading of them is more sophisticated:

If I could share with you a theological insight – and how difficult it is for people to live with it! The prophet whose name we don't know, but who is responsible for recalling Isaiah, puts it straight in Isaiah Chapter 45: 'I am the Lord . . . I form the light, and create darkness: I make peace, and create evil: I the Lord do all these things.' That's very strong. That is what oneness means. But in the Jewish prayer-book we find 'make peace and create all things'. To actually put it there in black and white that God creates evil is so difficult. But those who know their scripture know what the quotation says. And this is hard.

In a certain sense Auschwitz destroyed my childish notions. But it was in Auschwitz and some of the other camps I was in, in my teens, that my faith was forged. I understood then, and I understand this even better today, that Auschwitz was revelation, too. It was revelation of what happens when an evil principle is harnessed to up-to-date technology: I am prepared to say that was what humanity was asked to look at.

What happens, in fact, when you go all the way with

idolatry – for the Nazi system was nothing but an absolute giving yourself up to a wicked idol, with everyone willing to give everything including their souls to it and engaging in this obscene dance round their golden calf – and throwing innocent human beings onto its fires to keep it going.

What you cannot say is that God did it. It isn't true. People did that – Godless people, for Godly people cannot do that. Of course God was in Auschwitz. I believe God wept in Auschwitz. But you can't say God *did* Auschwitz. You cannot have it both ways. Human beings cannot say they have free will and then, when it gets out of hand, turn round and say 'Ah, but You did it!'

Free will is free will. There was a whole civilisation there. I know that many of my Christian friends ask themselves what must be an equally painful question. How could a Christian civilisation have failed after a thousand years or more in Central European Germany? Failed, to let this relapse take place into the most primitive and cruel fate? I am sure this is just as painful for both sides, but it is about *our* situation. And what does God do? I think God cries and says, 'My children, what are you doing? And what have you done?'

And, typically, Hugo Gryn went on to tell yet another of those rabbinical stories:

The rabbi is in his synagogue in a small village in Poland, at Yom Kippur – the Day of Atonement. And there is one man there, the tailor, who is apparently having the most dreadful argument – shaking his fists and muttering and everybody is disturbed by it but nobody likes to interrupt the service. But when it ends, the rabbi turns to this man and says, 'My friend, what on earth was going on there?'

'Ah!' says the tailor, 'I got into a terrible argument with God. I said to Him, Look, I know I am not perfect. There have been times when I sat down and had my meal without saying the blessing or the grace. And there have been days when I have hurried through my prayers. And to confess it, I have occasionally charged people for double thread when I only used single, and sometimes I have kept a bit of

cloth back to make clothes for my own children. So I'm
not claiming any special privileges. But you, God! You
take babies away from their mothers. Young men die on
the field of battle. People are cut down before their time
through illness. How can you let this happen? So let me
make a bargain with you. If you'll forgive me, I'll forgive
you.

And the tailor says to the rabbi, 'Did I do wrong?' And
the rabbi answers the tailor, 'My friend, you had such a
strong case – why did you let God off so easily?'

The point is, after we have blamed half our misfortunes on
ourselves or our fellow men and have accepted that we cannot
have both freedom of choice and freedom from human error, we
are still left with the other half of our sufferings which are
apparently beyond our efforts to avert – the disease, deformi-
ties, natural disasters. These can be further reduced in magni-
tude by arguing that it is increasingly in our power – if we have
the will – to foresee them, avoid them, cure them or at least
make them tolerable. But this is not much comfort to the
victims of the past, nor can we ever entirely eliminate the
undeserved suffering of the innocent in our own times.

Lord Fitt – Gerry Fitt, as most still think of him – was
hounded out of his native Ulster because he was a Catholic who
refused to condone violence as the only solution there. But
today he is inclined to think it is inevitable:

I believe that at the end of the day the divisions are so deep
that there isn't any hope of political reconciliation in
Ireland . . . I believe, the Sunningdale attempt having
failed (and now it's ten years on): well, I don't want to say
it in case I may be charged with precipitating it – but I
think we are in for a total bloody conflict in Northern
Ireland until one side beats the other.

Fitt does not believe that religion is the real basis of the
division in Ireland: only that by accident of history Catholicism
is worn as the badge of the native Irish, and Protestantism as the
badge of the 16th and 17th century Anglo-Scottish colonizers,
like feathers and hats in a Cowboys versus Indians campaign.

But as a devout and instinctive Catholic he is baffled to know what God is up to:

> Yesterday morning a magistrate and his wife and daughter were at Mass in St Bridget's chapel; and the killers – the young daughter was killed – were standing beside them in the Mass, taking part in the service, watching them. And as soon as they emerged from the chapel, the girl was killed and the father's been seriously injured. So you wonder to yourself, what part had God to play in that? I find that very hard to understand. And yet I accept it because I do believe in God.

And lest one retort, easily, that this was yet another case of God's heart being broken by the free wills of evil men, Gerry Fitt immediately went on:

> Even worse than Ireland – why does God let the terrible tragedy of the Third World happen? Why is God so generous to the Western World and why does He appear to be so hostile to so many millions of people who have committed no sin other than to have been born in Asia and the Upper Volta and the Gambia and India and Pakistan? I was at Mass recently and I heard the priest saying we were only born so that we could know, love, honour and serve God. Well, how do you reconcile that with a young kid that has happened to be born where they have these dreadful famines? If they were born to know, love, honour and serve God, that could be in conflict with the realities of it; because they live for a few weeks and then they die – they die of malnutrition, because they have no food. Someone once said, 'God must not have liked Africa and Asia. He must have had some spite against the coloured people.'

Well, is it or is it not a serious answer to say that we have the only possible universe; that having set it in motion, God cannot be forever tinkering with it; that having given us our freedom of will He cannot annul our choices; that in the very act of choosing, rightly or wrongly, we are forging our own souls? There are those who retort that we are so conditioned by our inheritance that any freedom left is derisory. But this is something the believer – particularly if he or she has had to make the choice whether to believe – will not accept. If the believer honestly contemplates the atheist or agnostic case, the believer must grant that the case is not so loaded on either side as to determine the outcome beyond question. And the outcome is hardly trivial.

There is a further conclusion which we have recently heard from Hugo Gryn, and it is one which has become widespread among the churches since the Second World War: that God Himself is 'in the mess', suffering with His creation, and that though we, like Job, may get no real answer out of the whirlwind the fact that God is there so transforms the situation that we turn from cursing to worship.

The impassibility of God has been part of the ancient teaching of the Church: that God, being beyond time and change, could not suffer and that nothing Man could do would make Him suffer. Muslims would certainly agree with that. But for Christians there is a widening flaw in it – the Incarnation, the claim that Jesus *was* God; for Jesus was also man (and not just a divine apparition) and Jesus visibly suffered and died. Jesus, we are told, wept. And if, even today, God is apprehended by most Christians as personal, and if He can love – that most vulnerable of relationships – how can He not also suffer? It is superficial to argue that God has no nervous system to hurt: many of our deepest human hurts do not come from having pins stuck into us. To speak of divine suffering is only to push the metaphor further.

The message of the Christian God is that we should not regard suffering as a defeat, but as a challenge to resurrection. I do not see it as a challenge that God deliberately and sadistically inflicts upon us (like the Wosbee commandant), but as one that He urges us to find in the inevitable setbacks of life. Frances Young, the theologian who has a grossly handicapped son, has drawn many positive dividends from the experience. But she is very careful to avoid any suggestion that resurrection is a magical 'one leap and you're free':

I remember vividly when I saw the ninth chapter of St John's gospel in an entirely new way. The story, you remember, is of the man blind from birth; and Jesus's disciples say to Him, 'Was it this man that sinned or his parents, that he should be born blind?' And Jesus gives an extraordinarily enigmatic answer to the effect that neither he nor his parents had sinned but this was done that the works of God might be made manifest in him . . .

Now this has always seemed to me to be an absolutely appalling statement. Why should that man go through all those years of blindness just so that Jesus could perform a miracle? And it was seeing that story in relation to the whole drama of the presentation of Jesus in St John which suddenly enabled me both to understand that story and to understand something of what my own handicapped child was about. It was the sense that this was a symbolic act, a parable of God's relationship with the world. The over-arching parable is Jesus Himself.

The coming of light into the world, the inability of the darkness of the world to respond and cope with it – the darkness has to snuff it out – this is the dramatic picture that comes through John's gospel. And yet, that moment when the light is snuffed out is the hour of glory in John's gospel, whereby the presence of God is actually found by His going into the deepest darkness. That is what Jesus means by 'I am the Light of the World', entering that deepest darkness. And He plays out being the Light of the World through the healing of the blind man.

Suddenly that all made sense and there was a level at which I was able to appreciate that it is very often in those deepest moments of darkness that people do actually sense the presence of God – and not when everything's going smoothly – that Jesus is a kind of demonstration of the presence of God in the darkness, and of God taking responsibility for the darkness.

Frances Young knows it is simply not realistic to expect her child to be healed miraculously. She does not claim that her positive dividends outweigh the negatives – 'There is no way you can do that kind of operation' – but having accepted the situation, there are constant reasons for giving thanks:

When people were testing me to see why I should be ordained as a minister, one of the things they came up with was 'What about your handicapped child?' And I remember saying, almost as an act of faith, 'He will be part of my ministry'. What I meant was that in all kinds of ways I had been formed and changed by having him, and that my perceptions had been deepened. But it came true in a way that was even more extraordinary than I could have anticipated.

One day I was visiting a number of church members in Birmingham, and I knocked on the door of a widow pensioner; and it turned out that she had a mongol grand-daughter. I was able to talk to her about that in a way that I guess no other minister had. Not long after that, I knocked on the door of a council house and it was opened by a black woman. We talked about families, and because it is an important and natural part of me to include my handicapped child, I mentioned him. She suddenly said, 'I've got a child like that, too'. It turned out that she had a child in a local hospital who had been there for a number of years. Nobody – not her minister or anybody in the congregation – knew about that child. She had been unable to share with anyone. And because I, too, had a handicapped child she had been able to tell me and share the agonies and problems and practical difficulties. There is a real sense in which, when people have had to go through their own valley of shadow, it can become something positive and creative in lots of ways that aren't possible without these experiences.

Perhaps the sceptic can still dismiss that kind of talk as the pietising of ordinary human decency. But Frances Young has had other encounters of far less practical value but of even deeper significance for her faith:

There was an occasion when I was visited by the minister of our church and he very gently suggested they were finding it very difficult to contain my son Arthur in the creche; because although he was still mentally a baby, physically he was very big and tended to be rather noisy – and the babies were disturbed. I could fully understand with my head, but I could not resist that terrible feeling of rejection, that the church was somehow turning Arthur out.

A day or so later, I had him in the wheelchair and I was pushing him to the local shops. And as I was passing the Catholic church, a crippled priest was hobbling along the pavement. And when he got level with us he stopped and spoke to me and to Arthur. (Arthur can't respond – he has no speech.) We just passed the time of day, and the priest said, 'How lovely to see him out and about!'

Now it was not a particularly dramatic or emotional experience. But I just knew afterwards that somehow that priest had embodied God and the Church, and it was a word of acceptance – that somehow I had been reassured that Arthur was part of the Church – whatever – that he was accepted by God – whatever – and that that priest had been (as it were) God speaking to me. He's probably totally unaware of the thing and doesn't even remember it.

In passing on that parable I am aware that I am not adding to the objective evidence for God. What I am trying to show is that in the streets and homes where God's supposed crimes are committed there are believers like Frances Young, Margaret Bowker (both highly intelligent women) and countless others of more modest attainments to whom they are not crimes at all – hardly blessings, perhaps – but events that are not beyond redemption thanks to their faith. This is not a glib or magical faith, but rigorous, strenuous and deeply realistic. It neither rejects nor glosses over the suffering and indignity, because it is based on the conviction that God Himself undergoes them along with us. He is asking us to go through nothing that He does not go through Himself. But He has all the advantages? I wonder. To recall Bishop John Vernon Taylor:

> I think God is engaged in a much longer and more dangerous adventure in which there is a great deal of accident around . . . That's the sort of world that God has submitted Himself to.

I could imagine, say, Don Cupitt snorting that God has submitted Himself to nothing (not that Cupitt snorts, actually).

I could imagine, also, some atheist complaining that the suffering God has only been invented as a last resort in recent years because the Great Jehovah in whom believers used to put their faith is no longer defensible. But it seems to me that the suffering God has always been there – we can see Him in the Bible through the patches in Jehovah's robes – and that it would be far more dishonest *not* to draw Him out than it would be to go on worshipping the punitive, impassible God.

Richard Harries, the Dean of King's College, London, would find it impossible to believe in a God who did not share human suffering; but at the same time Harries does not believe that God is entirely bound up with this world. In traditional terms He is transcendent (outside and above the creation) as well as immanent (within and alongside it):

> Of course, here we are groping for analogies and metaphors in order to talk about it. But I am certainly unhappy with one extreme form of modern theology which suggests that God and the world are totally bound up together. I think it is possible to affirm that God enters into human suffering, that He does that, and that it is only possible for Him to do it if in some sense He also stands outside the universe.

The theology which Harries is criticizing leads to the conclusion that God is a construction of the world and has no independent existence apart from it. But to say God was entirely independent would make it impossible for us to know Him. Another dilemma confronting the believer is that if he concentrates on the inner life of the spirit, he tends to become irrelevant to the world; whereas if he seeks an active expression of his understanding of God's will, he is liable to be dismissed as 'political'. Harries has no doubt that the Christian faith is primarily concerned with the old-fashioned saving of souls:

> But equally I have no doubt at all that this demands some kind of political expression as well. It is not possible in the modern world to love your neighbour unless that love includes the political dimension. Two hundred years ago it might have been possible simply to love your neighbour in person-to-person terms or through setting up a new

institution like a school or a hospital. But now society is so interdependent and complex that you cannot love your neighbour unless you are political. So I would want to affirm both the spiritual and the political, but with priority to the first and the second as the natural expression of it.

In view of this it was natural to seek out a Christian politician or two and ask how their faith did affect their worldly activities. Unbelievers often complain that believers are 'no better than the rest of us, and therefore hypocrites, because they ought to be', but this seems to me a feeble comment. I find that in some ways Christian politicians *are* better, or at least, when pressed, more honest about themselves; for the Church does not claim to be a congregation of the virtuous, it knows itself to be an assembly of sinners which is why it is there at all. To regard the profession of Christ as a declaration of virtue is outrageous pride; and to expect membership of the Church to work like a magic charm is the grossest superstition. Politics as we know it is *party* politics. If we look to God to tell us which party has His blessing and which His curse, we assume that He is prepared to write off thousands of His children on the basis of how they vote on nationalization or tax cuts. I doubt whether God has a manifesto position on either. So, as I put it to Shirley Williams – Roman Catholic and SDLP – should it make any difference to a politician whether he or she is a believer or not?

It ought to, because the graspable part of religion to me is the life of Christ. And I think what is so striking about it is that more and more often it throws up the answers to the way we live. It is so clear from the way in which the world has moved close to destruction that the old answers – the pursuit of success, the pursuit of material progress – are totally inadequate. They are leading us in all the wrong directions. It is only when you look at the teaching of Christ – and I suspect in things like the teaching of Buddha as well – that one finds the light. It is something to do with human beings living for one another; it is something to do with people's consciousness that they are part of a selfless society, that they do actually love one another without regard to being Christian or Jew, male or female, Greek or heathen, as St Paul said. Then one sees how the world might survive. How politicians behave ought therefore to be influenced by their awareness of the life of Christ.

Sadly, it so often is not. They divorce their beliefs from the way they actually behave as politicians. I don't think there is any argument that will stand up for saying the churches ought not to interfere in politics. What are they doing if they don't? Politics is what morality in daily life is called. That, to me, is what politics is all about. It is indivisible. You can't keep moral beliefs, religious beliefs, out of politics.

Mr John Selwyn Gummer, chairman of the Conservative Party and member of the General Synod of the Church of England, started out along surprisingly similar lines but moved in a rather different direction:

I do think being a Christian changes one's agenda. There are certain things which you cannot avoid facing, like our responsibility for the poorest in the community. Now, I may come with a different answer from other Christians, but I can't say that isn't an important question. Then there are certain issues which you are bound to look at different-ly. For example, if you think that every one of us is the child of God, I think you do have to have more concern for the individual and his importance than if you felt we could only be thought of as classes or masses or groups. And the third thing is that there are certain subjects – well, like abortion – where you have to agonise in a way in which you wouldn't if you did not have a belief in the soul and the fact that the individual's convenience must not be set against the life of another. So there are issues which are different.

I wondered why, if the Will of God were so important, Christian politicians seldom rose up in the House of Commons and prophesied in the name of the Lord?

I think it would be rather peculiar, wouldn't it? After all, if you are arguing about whether the amount of money available for the citizens of Liverpool and Manchester should go in one proportion or another, it is not often easy to see a direct Christian moral application . . . I think it is very difficult to see that there is a Christian view of politics which drops from Heaven and gives you all the answers. I don't think that's how God works. The whole story of the gospels is that He takes what you can give and transforms it. The small boy had to bring his loaves and fishes, although Christ could easily have fed the five thousand without any help from a small boy at all. And I think we are in the same position. We are expected to do what we can to understand, to decide, to bring our reason in the light of the Gospel, and those things come together and God transforms it. But the idea that God lets us off the hook from having to do the work, by telling us, 'Look – the situation is that the monetarists are almost right but not quite; and there is a little Keynesian matter you have to take into account . . .' I think that's a very odd view of God.

GP: But surely the teachings of Jesus about the rich and the poor are far more radical than your party – or any other party – dares to say?

Gummer: Well, it depends what you mean by radical, doesn't it? I happen to think that I belong to a very radical government. I think there is a tremendous amount of radicalism in saying, 'Let us change the nature of our society so that by encouraging enterprise and individual initiative we have the resources properly to look after the poorest'; and I am not sure that isn't very much in line with the Christian ethic.

GP: It still sounds to me like temporising. Jesus was really saying something much more revolutionary than that.

Gummer: Was He not saying the most revolutionary thing of all? Which is that each one of us is actually important because we are the sons of an Almighty Father, and that therefore we have a responsibility to Him for each other? He wasn't the first communist or indeed the first capital-ist. He was in fact saying something about human nature which is fundamental and revolutionary. But that is some-thing which no political party says, because that is not on the agenda of political parties. I am afraid politics is about this world, about making temporal decisions on whether

152 The Case Against God

we encourage Nissan Motors to go to one place or another. About whether we have tariff barriers against lima beans or not. Now these are matters to which Our Lord did not apply Himself, because that was not what He was talking about; and those who try to make Christ into a kind of politician demean themselves, I think, and Christ.

We might have wrestled on over the obligations of the rich and the renunciation of armed force, but there seemed little point. There will be more to say in the following chapter about the influence of the Church, but it is clear that while the awareness of God does illuminate and support the convictions of some politicians it is sufficiently fuzzy to serve left, right and centre. Which is probably just as well. For any one party to claim it was 'God's Own Party' would be intolerable, and for the divine signature to appear on any manifesto would be distinctly fishy.

One question that has bothered me throughout the investigation is this: If there is a God, He must surely be incomparably the most important thing in life. How, then, can He be so optional – something that people can manifestly take or leave as they choose? I hear now the calm, Scots voice of Ann Semple telling me:

> It's very much like a marriage. Unless I come as a free being and choose to have some kind of relationship with God, then it will have no meaning at all. There are clearly limits on all our freedoms. Some of us are much more limited than others – limited by deprivation, so that you are so concerned about getting by from day to day that you don't have much time for a spiritual dimension. To some extent we are all limited. Yet within those limits we still have freedoms, we still are able to make choices, and insofar as we are able – then we must choose.

But choose whether or not to believe in God? That suggested that either the choice was unfairly rigged or it was fairly unimportant. The city traffic ground past, spoiling our sound track, and I found myself asking crossly what God was doing for a place like Glasgow? Ann Semple answered:

I'm afraid that on occasions Christians are perhaps the best evidence around that God does not exist. I think that's because so few of us have actually worked out the implications of our faith in any but purely personal and devotional terms. We are very keen on personal sin and not so hot on institutional sin. I'm quite amused by recent criticisms from politicians of churchmen becoming involved in what they see as issues outside the spiritual realm. I cannot see there is a spiritual/secular divide. This is God's world, and if we claim to be Christians we have to be involved in the redemption of that world. As Christians we have to be involved in social and political action where the system is unjust and needs to be redeemed. That's something which Christians have traditionally been loath to do, and because of that I think we are open to criticism. We have to work at the system and chip away at the system as Christians. It isn't enough to sit back and say, 'Let's wait until everyone comes to God'. I'm not really interested in party politics. I don't think Christians necessarily have to be. But the Christian concepts of justice and peace are the base line from which we must operate in the political sphere.

And she went on to talk about famine relief, the elimination of leprosy, the laying on of clean water for the Third World – all possible if we would stop wasting our resources on nuclear weapons. It was the sort of talk, the tender-hearted clichés, that one expects from someone of Ann's youth; and yet it was sincere and very probably true and it is only having heard it so often but seen it so little that makes me call it a cliché. And I know that where I *have* seen those problems being tackled, there has almost always been a core of Christians at the heart of the effort, and they are people who have impressed me profoundly. Ann Semple may protest that believers are God's worst advertisement, but they are also His best. Whether that is true of the historic Church is another matter.

7

The Church in the Dock

'I think', said Paul Davies the physicist, 'that organised religion is in many ways one of the great evils that we have to live with. The Church has a lot to answer for; though in this day and age, at least in this country, it is a fairly inoffensive organisation, because it has become to a large extent depoliticised; but this is not true in other parts of the world.'

The poor old Church has not burnt anyone for ages (in fact it was usually the civil power which carried that out), and even though Professor Hans Küng has lost his licence to teach Catholic Doctrine he still survives comfortably enough and probably sells more of his books banned than unbanned. In Britain, at least, Catholics resort to birth control and divorce as freely as anyone else. So whatever the current sins of the Church, they are hardly on the scale of the mediaeval repression that still haunts people's memories.

Which is not to say the Church is now living up to the standards of its founders. Says Karen Armstrong, the former nun:

> If Jesus Christ or St Paul came down to earth today and were shown round the Vatican or even Canterbury, I'm certain they wouldn't recognise it as being anything whatsoever to do with them. I'm also certain that if it were pointed out to them that these institutions are based on what they gave us, they would be absolutely appalled and angry. Perhaps there would be a repetition of the incident where Jesus drove the money-changers out of the Temple.

> *GP*: Do you think we ought to blow the Church up and carry on without any Church at all? Do we reform it, or do we look forward to new churches?

Armstrong: The trouble is, people tend to get disaffected and leave the Church. Perhaps we shouldn't have left it. Perhaps we should organise demonstrations, strikes, go to Rome and lobby the Holy Father and make something happen. We're always told to sit back and accept things because that's good for our souls. But in fact Christianity throughout its history has been a revolutionary faith . . . But whenever it has got tied up with political establishment, it's gone downhill. The worst thing that happened to the Church was perhaps the conversion of the Roman Emperor Constantine. Perhaps revolution has got to come into the Church again, instead of all this triumphal, complacent wandering round saying, 'Here we are, Christians! Isn't this fantastic? Aren't we terrific people?' People don't want to be challenged by their faith. They want to be congratulated on it. And look at the Pope – being revolutionary in Poland, but nobody else in the Church is allowed to be political unless they happen to share his politics.

Revolution doesn't tie in with the Church of England, either. Think of a nice, tasteful evensong in the parish church. Very good ladies going in and arranging the flowers. They're not interested in revolution.

I do not, myself, meet much of the simplistic triumphalism that Ms Armstrong describes, nor do I feel entitled to take the flower ladies (who often *are* very good) by the throat and force the revolution upon them. Revolutions can be violent and destructive things. Reading back a little further, I agree the adoption of Christianity as the official state religion was a mixed blessing; but it was far from being an unmitigated curse. Nevertheless, Ms Armstrong is right: too many Christians do not feel challenged by their faith and, worse still, do not realise how the world is challenging it.

Downing Berners-Wilson is a retired Anglican clergyman with an intense interest in science, who realises that challenge all too well:

For many, the Church has become irrelevant. A boy once said to me (very politely): 'Sir, why should I sing the

Magnificat? I've never had a baby.' And it's true. It's nothing to do with him – it's irrelevant. It may be very relevant to someone who's pregnant, but not to a boy of fifteen. It's that sort of thing that makes me cringe.

We don't even say what we believe. We say we believe in the resurrection of the body – complete nonsense! We believe – at least I do – in the resurrection of the soul. Then why the hell don't we say so? I don't believe in the Trinity. You can't limit the Godhead, the whole of nature and the qualities of God into three persons. It requires a whole symphony of persons to get God exposed. It's this sort of thing that drives me round the bend! . . .

I certainly want to scrap the Creed. I want to bring it up to date with what we know about science and the body. We know the body doesn't survive. Open a coffin and you can see that in ten years.

GP: I'm afraid you are going to be accused of undermining the faith of simple people.

Berners-Wilson: Yes, I know. But I've never been concerned with the Christians. I've been concerned the whole of my life with those who cannot believe because of the things we have been talking about.

And with that I have much sympathy.

But God, if He exists, must find it irritating that His creatures spend so much of their time telling Him who He is instead of trying to hear what He wants and then doing it. It might seem to matter very little whether, of two people working on a community service project, one believed Christ was divine while the other did not. What they *do*, however, is not of the essence so far as the traditional Christian Church is concerned. The test of salvation is, do they both *believe* the *truth*?

We could struggle on for hours about the meanings of these two words alone, but I will try to cut things short. To believe something, especially in the religious context, is not quite the same as to know it: one is not claiming that it can be publicly demonstrated at will and beyond question. And to believe *in* something or somebody indicates a degree of *trust* that should even survive evidence to the contrary ('He trusted in God; let Him deliver him now, if He will have him: for He said I am the

Son of God'). It is, of course, hard to maintain such trust if it is persistently fruitless for no good reason; but belief in a personal God implies that such a superior person may know better than we do and cannot be treated as a kind of platform ticket machine – say the right prayer and get the inevitable blessing.

As for the truth, again in the religious context, this is not necessarily amenable to test demonstrations. The truth (for example, of the claim that the Eucharist is the Body and Blood of Christ) is not to be proved by chemical analysis: it is the reality, the ultimate significance of the situation, and although it may be a subjective reality compared with the presence of the cat in the garden, it is shared by a large enough number of people and has proved reliable enough for them now and in the past for the proposition to be taken very seriously. *Of course* it is a metaphor or simile. But it is a betrayal of the richness of human experience to deny expression to apprehensions which cannot be explained in chemical formulae. You can dismiss George Herbert's *Prayer* as, logically, nonsense; but you cannot argue the poem is untrue without revealing yourself as a spiritual cretin.

Marghanita Laski supplied me with a revealing footnote to this when I asked why she – an unbeliever – was so fascinated by the Christian faith:

> Because I am human. Because the Christian faith is the most developed religion the world has yet seen. It has a theology which is a very enticing form of intellectual exercise. It has been the cradle of all the great arts. How could I not be fascinated by the organisation which has satisfied so many human needs? We unbelievers, we've had only three or four hundred years and we have not sufficiently thought about these things, because we have been reacting against things. I remember saying to Freddie Ayer once, when we were on a Brains' Trust together 'What word do you use when you need to say what the religious call spiritual?' And he said, 'I've never felt any such need'. Now that seems to me to be odd.

But is it necessary, in order to use and enjoy the spiritual vocabulary, to become an obedient member of the institutional churches? Is there, in the grim traditional slogan, 'No salvation outside the Church', or is faith possible beyond it? Professor Owen Chadwick, historian of the Church, would very much like to think that it was:

> I would like to think it possible for Isaac Walton to sit on the bank of a stream and contemplate in silence the whisper of the leaves and the dot and flash of the water. The quiet is a vital element. He can come to see the glory and marvel in nature. And as he sees it, he is reaching outwards for something which is not explicable in material terms, and I don't think he needs a church for it.
>
> Secondly, I think that once he sees it, he starts to see also in human beings and his relationship to human beings – especially the sex relationship and family life – the whole way we have sought to understand God in terms of love. Well, that doesn't need a church either – it only needs a family. But I believe the fundamental act of religion is a solitary act: me and God; you and God.

We than had an argument about whether Professor Chadwick's religion was not too privatized and selfish, which ended with him agreeing that the New Testament Church was integral to Christianity:

> Nevertheless, I still believe the individual Christian doesn't need the Church to get between him and his Maker.

It so happens that my own religious practices, as a Quaker, are extremely private, unmoulded either by liturgy, sacraments or priesthood. I would as readily hoot at a bishop as I would at an organ-grinder. But I do regard myself as a member of the great universal Church (whether it accepts me or not) and, as I have written elsewhere, I value it for several reasons, not least because I think an entirely private religion can go seriously wrong, even mad. P. J. Kavanagh, the poet, reckons that he can arrange his own relations with the Deity:

> On the other hand, looking at the world suggests – does it not? – that ever since the Reformation, if people are given their heads, you end up with them very hungry and joining

the Moonies or whatever it is, believing anything rather than believe nothing. You get Hitler. People become communists for that reason (Communism is a form of religion, of course).

Therefore it has come to me comparatively late in life that there should be some social, communal expression of the faith. I think a body of traditional wisdom is extremely important. I personally get great nourishment out of communal ritual and being in a place with people with whom I have nothing else in common. I have noticed that when a nation is deprived of this there does seem a lack of nourishment.

Even Don Cupitt regularly celebrates the services of the Church of England and insists that there has to be a common language in religion:

You see, heretics need orthodoxy, otherwise their heresy would have no meaning; so there has to be a Church there, there has to be a mainstream of tradition. But there also has to be the attempt to find one's own voice, one's own religious identity vis-á-vis that tradition. You need the dialectic between the group and the individual. So I am reasonably happy with the Church of England, which I think is the most intelligent and up-to-date of churches in that it allows both: room for a strong tradition rooted in the whole of church history, and also a great deal of individual liberty to work out your own variation upon this traditional theme.

This sounds reasonable enough. It has always seemed to me that – if there is a God – He is a mountain which will look slightly different to each, according to where we stand at the foot of it, and which can legitimately be climbed by many different routes. Some may be broader or narrower, harder or easier, plainer or prettier than others; but what is the point of insisting fiercely that we must all use the same track?

Yet even within the up-to-date Church of England, as the recent nomination of Professor David Jenkins as Bishop of Durham showed – there are many who are outraged at the thought of a pastor who might not subscribe unreservedly to the creeds and had doubts about the literal truth of the Virgin Birth and the Resurrection. In part this must be ascribed to the conservatives' pride in truth for its own sake. In part also to their clerical dread of indiscipline. But in larger part I think it is due to a reluctance to accept the idea of *belief* and truth as I set them forth earlier. The notion that the credal statements must be accepted as literal and historical facts derives from the argument that they are based on the Bible and that the Bible is the Word of God. But that is a grossly oversimplified way of thinking.

For a start, the creeds themselves date from as late as the middle of the fourth century. They cannot possibly be claimed as representing the original faith of Christ and His apostles. As for the Bible being the Word of God – what can that possibly mean? Remember, we do not possess the original manuscript (if there ever was such a thing) of any book in either Testament. Are we claiming that God once dictated every line, supervised every editor and translator in every detail, so that instead of having a prayerful and inspired impression of His Will as those people sensed it, we have His precise rules and instructions for every contingency of our own day? That suggests a very pernickety and restrictive sort of God, which was not the God Jesus seems to have preached.

The Bible cannot be true simply because it *says* it is true – though if you do believe that, you are very hard to assail. The Bible, it seems to me, is a relentless and impressive movement *towards* truth: Isaiah had a much clearer vision of God than the patriarchs, and Jesus a clearer vision still (though His disciples kept misunderstanding Him). A firm evangelical will insist that all we need to know of God has been revealed to us already. But have we understood it right? Admittedly there would be no Christianity without the testimony of the apostles – however second or third hand. But have they, has the Church, got it right? I put this to David Winter, a very firm but very reasonable evangelical, who runs radio religion at the BBC:

Of course our system of belief has to be handed down, and it seems to me a ludicrous idea that every believer down the centuries should be expected to have a clean sheet of paper and work out the faith for himself from scratch. I think some of the troubles we are getting ourselves into this century, with this constant redefinition, is that it seems to be suggested that everyone should write their own creed.

On the other hand, everybody has to make it their own. And I suppose the test of it really is: Here is this system of belief – here is the Christian picture of God – here is the Jesus insight – now try it! Put your faith in it, because it works! And my guess is that if it did not work for people – if faith did not speak to faith – then it would have died out a very long while ago.

GP: You're telling me that in order to believe, you've got to believe. That's just tautologous, isn't it?

Winter: But it isn't irrational belief. I said faith speaking to faith. I think what we are doing is responding to God, and that all belief in Him is response to Him, and that the initiative comes from God. The two great propositions of the Judaeo-Christian tradition seem to me God exists – God speaks. The two must go together. If God exists but He hasn't said anything, then He's a monster. But if He has said something – how can I find it out?

A vital part of the answer is to rely on the Christian record:

Not only as it is written, but as it has been lived out in the Christian community, the Church. As it is experienced by people who believe. I think you have got this strange, experiential element of knowing Jesus *now* – of feeling you have some relationship with God through Him which helps you to understand what the Jesus Story and the Bible means . . .

We'll never know perfectly. To me believing does not just mean accepting things as they are handed on to you. But within the believing community, it feels different. And that's why I think the Church's role in interpreting the Christian revelation is tremendously important. I'm very suspicious of anyone who sets up a rival show – a private show – and says, 'I've just hit on a completely new understanding of the gospels'.

I admit that it is unlikely, after all these years, that anyone would hit upon a completely new key that opened up the faith. I admit, too, that it is unlikely seventy generations of Christian believers have been totally deceived. Even David Winter concedes there is a certain circularity about the case, but there are other reasons for being convinced by it. Richard Harries, who is far less evangelical, finds the canvas painted by church doctrine to be overwhelmingly *beautiful*:

> I think the idea of a God who became incarnate and died upon the Cross and rose again, and who has our good in mind not just now but for eternity, is literally the most beautiful idea that has ever been thought of. Of course, because it is beautiful that doesn't mean to say it is bound to be true. But if it hadn't got that kind of sheer attractiveness, that compelling power, I don't think that I would myself be able to believe in God. It is the sheer, sublime attractiveness of the total scheme of Christian doctrine that really does draw and impel me. I know the idea of doctrine is very dry to most people and puts them off religion. But it is precisely the opposite to me, because it is Christian doctrine that defines the kind of God that I believe in.

This is very like the delight of a mathematician at the *elegance* of a theorem, or of a musician at the successful resolution of a symphonic movement. The thing makes sense within itself, everything checks and balances, it gains power from its own consistency. But a faith that is lived cannot, after all, be a self-confirming word-game. It impacts upon events and events collide with it and somehow the two must be able to live together. There are many sincere believers who feel they can still achieve this, but that when they try to define their faith it no longer accords with the elegant, traditional patterns of the Church.

David Keddie is a minister of the Church of Scotland who has been carpeted by his presbytery and accused of undermining the Kirk:

> And yet the more I talk to these people with the so-called 'simple faith', I find that their faith is not simple at all. It's

a faith they very often have to adjust and occasionally abandon because of what's happened to them – because their simple faith couldn't cope with some of the problems and mysteries they had. What I have always wanted to do is simply to say to people, 'Whatever your faith is, it belongs in the Church. You shouldn't ever feel that you've got to put yourself outside of the Church because you don't share the certainty that you think your fellow Christians have. In fact, if you ever talk to them you might discover that they weren't as certain as you thought they were.'

If faith can't cope with the kind of things that I'm saying, then it's not really living, versatile, dynamic faith at all. I do believe in the Church. Not in any one particular institution or manifestation of it. But I believe in the Church. And I'm desperately concerned for people outside the Church, because it seems to me the gulf between the Church and the outside is hardening in our age. It used to be very blurred round the edges – it's becoming much harder. I want people outside to come into the Church and bring their gifts with them – their doubts, their certainties, their sorrows and joys, their minds and their creative capacities – and I want them to deploy these in the service of the Church and the community, in response to Christ. And they won't come in.

Now I can only speak out of the West of Scotland experience. People think there's a kind of Identikit Christian, and unless you can be that you can't belong. Now, if I go to a gathering and it becomes known I am a minister, the religious discussion is unleashed by people who are desperate to talk about all kinds of things – superstition, black magic, that kind of thing – but they want to talk to a minister who is prepared to talk to them. They say to me, 'My minister never preaches about this kind of thing'.

So if people write in and say, 'You're destroying my simple faith', then I would say first of all, 'Is your faith living, or is it a way of escape – a protective shield you're putting round yourself – and you don't question it?' I want to broaden the appeal of Jesus to those who cannot see Him because the Church and the traditional received imagery get in the way. I would want to say that there's more to Jesus than perhaps they realise.

Unless the Church can get its belief and its symbolic language and its worship in tune with the kind of world in which we are living, the Church will deserve to pack up. The Church is often dead in people's eyes – thus confirming that Christ is dead. So I consider myself to be infinitely more evangelical than the people who claim to be evangelical.

Frankly, I like that kind of talk. But if, in Britain, you look for a congregation which is full of growth and enthusiasm you are most unlikely to find it led by a minister like David Keddie. You are much more likely to find it in the hands of an admirer of Billy Graham or – here and there – of a traditional Anglo-Catholic. I doubt, myself, whether these can withstand the gales of secularism; and despite the talk about 'not counting heads' or of 'bottoming out' and 'starting the slow climb back' it seems to me that the over-all decay of church membership continues. The survivors are rearranging themselves into smaller, keener groups, but the broad reasonable middle of the road is becoming emptier and emptier.

As so often, the experience of the United States points the way. Paul Heelas, of Lancaster University, agreed that just as Reaganite politics and Reaganite religion seemed to go hand in hand, so would Thatcherite politics and religion. But America always has its special features:

The picture is that mainstream denominations are tending to lose their clientele, but that two movements are booming. One is the Pentecostal-Charismatic-Fundamentalist end of the spectrum. The other is the area known as the New Religious Movements, who seem to be doing very well indeed. Most of their clientele are middle-class college-educated, aged between 18 and 30, who in the vast majority of cases have been exposed to a rationalistic if not scientifically orientated education. And yet they are joining religions which, by and large (but not entirely) are rejecting both the technological standard and the value of rationality. Most of these new religions mount fully-fledged assaults on the rational mind. Most of them hold that it is only when one has ceased to identify oneself in terms of one's social ego and rational mind that one is going to experience enlightenment or revelation and start living in terms of one's true nature.

Heelas went on to make a spirited defence of one such movement – EST or Erhardt Seminar Training (which includes selling things by telephone among its activities) and concluded:

> In terms of the accusations which are made against these organisations – brainwashing, fascist authoritarianism, a turning away from the real issues of the day, psychiatric casualties and so forth – these accusations seem to me ill-founded.

But did they actually have any room for a God? Not as a transcendent being with whom one could enter into a relationship and whom one should worship; more of an 'immanent universal self'. There would be no doctrine or mythology about this because, 'beliefs are what prevent one from coming into contact with this source – beliefs are in many ways the enemy'. It struck me that while my style of looking for God could be criticized as too intellectual, *this* style went too far in the opposite direction.

So, for all its faults, I went back to the Church and talked (as I did not often do in this investigation) to a few bishops. True they have a vested interest in the subject, but in my experience they are all too ready nowadays to admit the Church's faults. Said John Vernon Taylor of Winchester:

> I think it has not claimed too much, but sometimes claimed it in too strident a tone of voice. All through the history of the Church the great theologians (if one can understand them) are actually saying this constantly. Aquinas, Augustine, one after another the great voices are talking about the unknowable. And yet *enough* is known, and it is known with enough strength and joy of overwhelming discovery, that in proclaiming that joy and discovery the Church is almost bound to speak with a tone

of conviction. Sometimes it sounds like overconfidence . . .

Certainly our more childish and inadequate pictures of God have rather been taken away; and in the long run I think that is probably healthy for us all. Because I have always believed that God withdraws Himself when He realises that you have an inadequate picture of Him – so you can lose that picture, with all the pain that is involved. And then wake up and stretch out and through a period of uncertainty come to a truer image of Him – find something more real. And then even that may be taken away, and you go on to find something even more real.

In a village in Oxfordshire I found Lord Blanch, the former Archbishop of York, complaining that the God presented by the Church as he knew it was often nonexistent:

Sometimes all we represent is a God who is more concerned with putting Anglo-Catholics up and Evangelicals down; or adhering to particular values which are the product of history rather than theology, which divide us all. Whereas when I move in the secular world, I find quite a lot of people who express dim feelings of longing and hope which are infinitely more real than some of what we might call orthodox religion.

GP: So do we let God go secular and not bother about the Church?

Blanch: Can't stop bothering about the Church, any more than you can stop bothering about Israel, really. I believe it to be called of God, just as Israel was. It is absolutely essential because I believe it represents a theological framework and an intellectual structure within which we have to work. I believe it still has enormous values in the world, as is evident in times of great need or distress, or the great festivals of the Christian Year – they still speak to people. So I don't minimise the importance of the Church, but I would hope to see it as representing the face of God rather better.

I remembered that just as his brother of Canterbury, Robert Runcie, had been a Guards tank officer, Stuart Blanch had flown as a wartime navigator with the RAF. It was strangely impressive that men who had been through such savagery should have gone on into the Church:

Actually, the experience of being involved in a service where people you knew were dying around you had the effect on me that it had on many aircrew: that it gave them a vivid sense of their mortality here on earth. And, although it sounds childish, it made them perhaps aware of the realities which they had never experienced before, or never thought about. There was a disproportionately large number of men in the Air Force who, as a result of their experience, were later ordained. It really is quite a remarkable number. So the intellectual difficulties of the faith remain and always do. But the wartime experience did nothing to dissuade me from faith, and the experiences I had in the Air Force did actually contribute to it.

It would be surprising to find a bishop (even a retired one) who denied that we needed the Church. But I have never been convinced that Jesus intended anything like it; and when I came to my next bishop – Michael Hare-Duke of St Andrews, who lives by the pleasant waters of the Tay – I wondered out loud whether, in fact, *God* needed the Church:

I sometimes wonder, too. Of course there has got to be some vehicle in which the hopes and dreams and stories are carried – that's really what the Church is. But when the Church gets it all wrong and takes itself so appallingly seriously and doesn't see that it's just that – but feels it is the Ark of Salvation – then I think it has got it totally wrong.
  Because God is the Saviour, the Church is not. We simply tell the story. We open it out for human beings, as Jesus Himself opened out the stories and left people. We all think our own systems are right, and we become ludicrous; because at that point we cease to be the people who've got a story to tell; we become the purveyors of the system. My system becomes right and your system becomes wrong, and then it becomes more important to stop you getting away with your system than it is to tell the

story. And at that point the Church seems to me to lose all its credibility and to have sold out on the God it proclaims.

Bishop Hare-Duke returns constantly to this view of the Christian religion as a treasury of story-telling, and I must say it appeals to me as reflecting a God who reveals Himself not through commandments carved in stone but through human activities which we are to interpret for ourselves.

But yet again, do we really need a paid, professional, hierarchical Church for that? After two thousand years, is the world any the better for organised Christianity? David Winter insists that it is:

> I think Christianity has made the world a very great deal better than it was before. I think you have only got to travel from the so-called decadent West to any other country of any other religion and ask yourself whether it really is preferable. If you think of the advance of Europe through Christianity, and then as it spread to other countries – if you think of the beginnings of orphanages, hospitals, schools, the fact that the weak in society ought to be cared for: however much it was done in a paternalistic or patronising way, it was done. And as far as I can see nobody else had ever thought it was worth doing before. With all its faults, Christianity has actually contributed an enormous amount in art and beauty, in civilisation and in personal freedom and justice, even though it has taken a very long while.

Shirley Williams felt much the same:

> When one looks at the way the churches have, from time to time, been in the grip of corruption and power going to their heads, I think the sheer survival of the institutions says something remarkable about Christianity (and one could say the same about Judaism as well, I think). So we *are* better off in terms of the institutions. If you're asking is the *world* better off, I think I would simply say the battle between the children of light and the children of darkness has been entered into on a much larger battlefield than any we have seen before; but I would certainly not say that the

children of light are weaker in this generation than they were two thousand years ago.

The easy mistake to make in judging God by His Church is to think the Church means bishops and priests and doctrines. It does not. It is the whole congregation of the faithful, of whom the clergy are the servants and not the masters; though too often the laity offer themselves to be mastered and resist the invitation of the more enlightened clergy to take responsibility for their own faith. This is not the place, I think, to discuss organizational reforms; I doubt if the Church would become more inspiring if, for example, it had even more committees and synods, or if it went back to the 1662 Prayer Book and the Mass in Latin. I suspect that its present eclipse has something to do with the mediocrity of its ministers (those quoted here, of course, excepted), and that that in turn has something to do with the meaninglessness of the profession and the feebleness of its intellectual content. The ablest ministers I have met came to their ministry after having forged their faith elsewhere. Nor were they all ordained, for Christians can minister to their fellows in a thousand ways from parenthood to shopkeeping, teaching, journalism, delivering the post – in any way that serves with love because they believe it to be the will of God. It is such people that make the Church admirable at all, such people who have achieved the miracle of the Church's survival, and such people who to me are the most cogent evidence that God exists. The variety of their faith has been essential to me in getting some idea of the richness of this God. Atheists who often demand that believers should affirm the unbeliever's image of God have no idea of the private heterodoxy that goes on in the heart of the average believer, and yet does not demolish his or her faith. I sometimes wonder whether the average priest or minister realises that either; but he would be sadly mistaken if he thought he was doing God or the Church a favour by trying to bring it all into line.

But now I am drawing to the end of my evidence and it is almost time to reach a verdict and to pass sentence. But upon whom?

8

Verdict and Sentence

As I was beginning this chapter, a letter appeared in *The Times* from the Reverend Professor E. L. Mascall concerning the supposed heresies of the new Bishop of Durham. The issue, wrote Professor Mascall, was whether the occurrence of Jesus in history 'has brought about a change in the objective condition of the universe or only in the subjective outlook of Christians'; or, in simpler terms, 'Has Jesus made a change in the way the world really is, or only in the way that it is helpful for us to think about it?'

The reason why no thoughtful believer can answer this question is that we are not sure what the Reverend Professor means by 'the objective condition of the universe' or 'the way the world really is'. *Objective* and *really* look like good solid terms that no faithful Christian should deny, while *subjective* and *helpful* look shifty and wet. Yet the Professor cannot be saying there was any measurable difference in the universe as a result of Christ's life, death and resurrection; that the world felt hotter, colder or even safer as a result. He must be talking about theological, metaphysical or spiritual reality, which is much harder to pin down. But because he values the achievements of Christ so highly, he is anxious to discourage people from thinking that 'the effects are whatever you think they are'.

I happen to think that the effects of God suffering in Man at the hands of Man are powerful and continuous and always have been; that they are far too vigorous to be confined in a single doctrine; but that they have been most visibly broken through to us on the Cross, where, among other things, God is saying 'I am like this; and I am *so* like this that, so far as you are concerned, I *am* this'. I think that is objectively true only in the sense that it is always available to us, whether or not we choose to accept it – choose to make it real by realising it; but to say that it works 'objectively' for those who reject it, that it works for them independently of their choice, seems to me to be saying something very odd. It assumes a universe (a spiritual universe) in which Man is not, after all, free to choose to reject God. And if one thing is clear to me as a result of this investigation, it is that – if there is a God – we must be able to deny that there is. God would not be the God I believe Him to be if we could prove that He was.

I embarked on this rigmarole about Professor Mascall's letter not because it is really part of the case for or against God but because it shows, once more, that we cannot confront the Age of Disbelief by talking to it as if it were the Age of Belief when we could still use words like *real* and *objective* in our religious discussions without being misunderstood. It is not my purpose now to go deeper into the significance of the Cross; which may disappoint those believers whose access to God is precisely through that event. Such people are greatly blest already and probably have no need of the sort of arguments I have been conducting. But I am aware of another audience – I suspect a much larger one – which either has its own heretical views of Christ or finds the various dogmatic views of Him on offer a positive discouragement to faith. Without a view of Christ as *somehow* divine I do not think one can get very far along the Christian way or share in its insights. But there are many people who either do not believe in God at all or do not believe He matters very much (for He seems to do nothing of any consequence) or, on the other hand believe quite definitely in a God of all religions and disapprove of what they see as Christian attempts to monopolize Him. It is this disorganized and rather secretive audience which I am trying to engage most of all.

Does God exist? To declare myself, as equivocally as ever, I will say that I hope I believe – I know that I trust. I agree with Richard Swinburne that reasonable inductive argument does establish a high degree of probability that God exists. It cannot establish that He doesn't. I find the scientific arguments against Him – Free Lunch and all – too provisional and incomplete to shut Him out; while the indications that observers are *necessary* for the universe and that we have the precise and only universe needed to produce *us* seem to me to be of awesome significance. Witnesses kept pointing out that we could not assume we were the only conscious beings in the universe and must not jump to the conclusion that it was all for our benefit. But we still have not contacted any other such beings, nor they us. What if that continues indefinitely?

Added to such intellectual exercise I have my own inner experience: not so dramatic as some I have quoted, but to me well worth following up *as if* there were a God. Added to that again, the impressive witness of the many believers I know, of all faiths, both quoted and unquoted in these pages. Put together within the structure of the Christian faith and developed along liberal theological lines (though not, I think, as radical as Don Cupitt's), I find it works – it makes sense – it is well worth going on with and I could not be without it; though it is not yet finished and I should be suspicious of it if it ever were. For there is always the possibility that I may be wrong: not so much that there is *no* God (though that can never be wholly eliminated) but that He is drastically Other than what I thought.

In some senses, He must be. For if He exists He must be far beyond our comprehending and we can never close the ring around Him. He has the quality of moving all the time so as to draw us in pursuit, and He must always have room to escape our clutches. He is not this, not that, not the other. Because of this, we cannot convincingly say what we mean by 'God'; none of our strait-jackets will fit. He is, to quote Rowan Williams, 'the connections we cannot make' but which we believe to be there. And there are still the enormous mysteries into which He vanishes from time to time, only to re-emerge on the far side.

I have said, several times, that God is strangely optional. What I really mean is that He is, by His very nature, essential; but that our belief in Him is optional; we do not *have* to believe in Him. I think this has something to do with His character as Love. Love, to be complete, has to be recognized for what it is and where it comes from, has to be responded to and returned, or it is not Love at all – or only Love frustrated. But that response must be voluntary. If it were compulsory or automatic it would be uncreative and not worth having, merely impersonal servitude; and that is not the relationship which the Christian believer, at any rate, senses. He feels himself to be known, addressed, commanded and loved – as a person. But he or she is also aware of being able to reject all of this. Indeed, Sin is the very awareness of having done so.

But the awareness of God's existence would have little point if it were only beautiful and true. It must also have some practical value, and we have heard many witnesses explain what that is for them. We have also heard unbelievers explain how they manage perfectly well without it; but I was wryly amused to find how many of them were aware of what they lacked and anxious to find a respectable substitute. They sensed the importance of religion to art, culture, morality, the human urge for pattern and ritual in life. Many of them were also aware how brittle and fallible the substitutes have proved.

I think we are in grave danger from atheism and idolatry in their various forms, whether the worship of the state, the class, the party, pleasure, possessions, power. It sounds trite, but I think it becomes steadily truer; for what we are seeing now is not only the collapse or forcible preservation of the political, economic and scientific idols that have been erected, but also the disillusion and despair of the emptiness beyond. Now that so many people have lost the language and mythology of godly religion, they hardly know how to handle such religious apprehensions as they do have, and they are tempted to embrace complete irrationalism including (it should be said) the use of drugs.

Most addictive drugs do mimic or parody certain of the effects of religion, and most religions – knowing this – have battled with the impostors. It is ironic that unbelievers should condemn faith as being fantastic and unreal, not only because believers find it to be quite the opposite, but because the substitutes, whether chemical or political, produce those very qualities. Often they have a degree of cruelty and unreason scarcely approached by the worst excesses of religion. And this is because, as the great Elizabethan, Richard Hooker, put it, 'Unless the last good of all, which is desired altogether for itself, be also infinite, we do evil in making it our end'.

I wrote that we cannot convincingly say what we mean by

God, but that does not stop us from trying and from producing some quite exotic descriptions of Him. Increasingly these incorporate a feminine element, as if trying to make up for the lost centuries when sexuality was unclean and the holy could only be touched by men. The feminine has always been there as a handmaiden, most prominently in the cult of the Virgin Mary, but attempts by people like the Gnostics and Cabalists to place it at the heart of the Godhead were invariably stamped out, or at least swept under the carpet. It is a deeply mystical concept, often conceived as the Holy Wisdom, the Bride of the Word; and among Jews it is the *Shechinah*. Penina Peli, wife of a Jerusalem rabbi, has even seen the *Shechinah* in a vision:

> I think all being is God, all being that is creative. God stands for creativeness as against negation of existence, or destruction. God's presence in the world is the *Shechinah* – the Hebrew word for the feminine presence of God who should dwell in Jerusalem on the Temple Mount. That's the Shechinah's main address, in a temple that should be open to all people who believe in the same God, with the Jews as the priests, but not as a favoured people. And this presence restored in the world will somehow bring about what I call a spiritual ecology of the fullness of God's abundance. So God has got masculine and feminine. The feminine lives on the earth and the masculine is the unseen God.
>
> My youngest daughter got married last week. We went to the Wailing Wall – I haven't told this to anyone yet – and I looked up at the Temple Mount, and I had a sense of the Shechinah weeping and yearning to be there again, and to be welcomed by all those who believe in God. And I began to cry. I think that as real an experience as I've had. It just happened last week. I really felt such a yearning and longing.

GP: What does the Shechinah look like?

Peli: Radiant, bringing blessing, life, I suppose. There are different associations in the Bible, and they are mostly to do with light, because light is the most physical expression of good and blessing.

That kind of vision might be acceptable to a Catholic mystic, but not, I think, to a Bible-based Protestant, nor to a Muslim – who would not accept the Protestant's image of God incarnate in Christ. Are they really talking about the same God at all? Gai Eaton described to me the feelings of an Arab friend of his, a distinguished Islamic scholar, who had spent several years studying the Christian faith:

> He said: What baffles me is this: Christians are told that God created the world by an act of His Will, and yet He chose to make His perfect creation – Man – corrupt almost from the start. Apparently He was not powerful enough to correct this corruption, except by begetting a Son and sending the Son to be killed to save mankind. And my friend said: Now to me that seems like a case of God playing games with Himself, and God does not play games. I think that is the best summing up I've heard of the basic Muslim attitude: God does not play games.

I suppose the Christian answer to that would be: It is not God that plays games with us, it is we who insist on playing games with Him. We are back with free will – our freedom to choose to defy Him – and the wonder is, perhaps, that it has not destroyed us long ago. The Christian would say that the only reason why it has not is the process revealed by the Cross. Some believers see this as an old-fashioned sacrifice, vicarious suffering on behalf of sinners, God paying the penalty that cannot be withheld from His own justice. But others are more inclined, nowadays, to see the Cross as a sign – an immensely potent one – of how God absorbs the evil inflicted upon Him, forgives, and redeems the disaster by bringing good out of the evil. That is not so much playing games as working a miracle. Or as John Vernon Taylor sees it, an enormous adventure:

> For me, it all stems from the truth that God is Love. In the being of the Trinity there was Love and reciprocal Love, there was no need for anything else. But because of the overflowing nature of that Love, I believe that God set about the extraordinary adventure of creating that which was not God – creating His other – which would give back the same sort of Love.

So it seems to me, the whole story of creation is a slow, slow story of bringing into being the environment within which Love could emerge. Now, straight away, once you have said that, you have laid the agenda for an enormous process of creating freedom, of creating accident, of creating courage, endurance, and even before that the first beginnings of consciousness, awareness, until you get the sort of sensitivity that can respond and move on towards the emergence of love.

I think that even within the range of the Bible, which is very recent history, you can see something which is hardly Love developing towards Love. So that when Jesus talked about a new commandment, it really was almost new in the history of the world – Love of that quality. And I think God is still working on that enormous adventure and it is fantastically costly. But somehow, for Him, for the ultimate result of a reciprocal Love, it is worth enduring the Cross; and what seems worse, it seems to be worth condemning creation to the Cross because of the ultimate revelation and resurrection of Love which will emerge.

Which suggests that God *is* playing games with us – that we *are* victims of a cosmic Wosbee – for we never asked to come on this 'adventure'. But I think again of the rabbi, the poet and two or three other witnesses who said, in effect, 'Why are we always complaining that life isn't easy enough? We deserve *nothing*. Life on any terms is good'. And I think of Richard Swinburne telling me:

If the world was so made that there was nothing to be improved in it, no evil to be removed from it, then God would not have given to conscious beings a serious alternative as to what to do with the world. He would have taken all the decisions back into His own hands. Though there might be something to be said for this, there is quite a lot to be said for giving conscious beings that choice.

It is an enormous responsibility He gives to those beings, and in particular humans. But then He's prepared to trust them – like as a Father trusts his children – without dictating to them what to do, and allows them to do what is bad. So God does. But I think that is the greatest gift He can give to any being – freedom of choice. And He gives us serious freedom of choice by allowing there to be evils around which we can ameliorate or remove.

GP: But I can imagine, say, a deformed baby, as it grew up, saying 'Thanks a lot for nothing, God!'

Swinburne: Yes, he has plenty of opportunity for resentment – that is among the freedoms that God gives people – freedom to nurture resentment. It would be difficult, of course, to *say* this to the baby as he grew up: but, nevertheless, objectively speaking, he has so much to be grateful for, simply for living. If he can move one arm and everybody else can move two, it is, I think, very wrong of him to resent the fact that he can't move the other. He should rather concentrate on the fact that he can move one arm. Of course, you could put even harder cases to me. Philosophers who sit in armchairs perhaps have less experience of those hard cases than many others do. Nevertheless, insofar as there is a conscious being, capable of thoughts, capable of choices about what to do, that is something to be grateful for.

Like Professor Swinburne, I am hesitant to hold up the suffering as magnificent examples of the goodness of God – it is not the suffering but what can be done with it that really provides His opportunity. But I heard too many examples of precisely that to be able to brush it aside. Said Shirley Williams:

The greatest privilege of being a politician is that one has immediate access to a tremendous range of people; and when I have really seen God working is in the astonishing courage and magnanimity I've come across in individuals. I've seen on a number of occasions the amazing courage of people faced with learning that they are going to die. The way in which that, instead of ruining or cramping their lives, enables them to go quite beyond themselves in the way they think about other people – their generosity – the way in which they try to prevent other people suffering because of their own suffering. One really does see them pick up the Cross of Christ – some who don't even know that's what they are doing.

David Bellamy, the botanist, gave me another example which I am not sure I like so much:

> I have lived with a number of primitive cultures and they all look to some Spirit beyond their understanding. There were these people in South America – much better natural historians than I am ever going to be: they totally depended upon the Amazon rain forest in which they lived, yet they had a very strong concept of God. In fact, this particular tribe, when the Father died, the child would be buried alive with the Father under drugs. And I asked this particular child through an interpreter, 'Now, come on, you know you are without doubt the favourite child. When your Father dies, you will die too.' I would still love to know whether it was the interpreter saying this – but I think it was the child – she said, 'But I go to a better place where it never rains and where there is always food, and I go with my father.'

Not a very Christian practice, I admit, and only marginally better than burning a widow on her husband's funeral pyre. But it does show how people who are closer to nature than you, my urbanized readers, find nothing unreal about the unseen. They find evidence of the divine kingdom all about them.

Then why does the atheist not see this evidence? Perhaps he does, but simply interprets it differently, for he has the freedom to do so. Father Jack O'Brien of the Jesuits grants that:

> Everyone has to grow up and have their own experiences in their own way. I think this is why, ultimately, you can't ever win an argument between a believer and a non-believer. It doesn't really come from arguments; I think it comes from experience and how one evaluates experience. Supposing you never ask the key questions?
>
> I remember one night I was walking on the campus back in Montreal. A beautiful dark night with no moon, and suddenly I heard a very loud noise. And I looked up, and against the sky I could see the wedge – all the birds heading south. And I think I'll remember that for the rest of my life. How do they know? Do you mean to tell me this is chance?

GP: What about genes or geomagnetism?

O'Brien: If all that came into place without any Creator putting it there – then that's chance.

On the one hand you can argue that the odds against the universe coming together by chance are so huge as to be impossible; on the other that, given a basic principle or two, it is inevitable. But the religious question has never really been *How?*, it is really *Why?* The unbeliever can only respond that it is an improper question: that there is no *Why?* But the believer finds it impossible to accept there is a whole dimension of his being seeking an answer to a question if there is nothing for it to work on. He has eyes because there is something to see, ears because there is something to hear. Does he not therefore have religious apprehension because there is a God to apprehend? He may tell you that what he apprehends is an old gentleman with a long white beard or Three in One and One in Three, but that is only his way of expressing the few small fragments of God that he can get hold of.

Is it possible, then, that we might get hold of still more? That we might further develop our understanding of God, just as we can see it developing through the Bible and beyond? (For, remember, the doctrine of the Trinity is a later development, nowhere to be found in the Old or New Testament.)

This is dangerous ground to tread; and the adventurer is sternly warned off it by those who insist that Scripture, and perhaps the Church, have already given us all we need to know for salvation. The Bible, of course, is so rich and so demanding of interpretation that it is possible to find grounds for almost any theology one wishes to embark upon, from Liberationism to Feminism. More subversive in the end is the so-called Reductionist approach, which tries to reduce complicated ideas always to simpler ones. Intellectually there is nothing dishonest about this (quite the reverse) but the tendency is to become *too* intellectual, to inhibit the emotional richness of the elements in faith, and in the end to present faith not as people actually hold it but as it is reckoned they *ought* to hold it. This, I suspect, is the way Don Cupitt is going:

For me, the Christian God is the Father of Jesus Christ. And insofar as I live like Christ and share His values and my life is orientated in the way His was, then I believe in His God. And when Christ says (or rather, the Christ of St John's gospel says), 'I am the truth', what He is saying is 'Live this way, share these allegiances, and you will have something you can rely on, something that will not let you down'. So the values, the idea of God, Christ Himself – these things are data and they do help us. What is wrong is to go on to mythologise that into the superstitious picture of an invisible person behind the scenes. That seems to me an illusory idea.

But from my observations, there are countless people claiming to be Christians who are very well aware that they do *not* live like Christ but who would be justly incensed to be told that they had a superstitious picture of God. To them He is not just 'an invisible person behind the scenes' but also an invisible person very much on stage. They may have to construct the way they express Him, but they are quite sure that what they experience is something given from outside their own natures. As we have heard, that kind of experience is neither so rare nor so neurotic as sceptics believe, and people who have systematically studied it are amazed at our refusal to take it as serious evidence. The trouble is that many people still regard religion as a form of magic which, if true, ought to produce tangible results to order: cures, miracles, prophecies, all the party tricks which no self-respecting God would stoop to if He knew His own will.

Don Cupitt quoted a text – 'I am the way, the truth and the life: no man cometh unto the Father, but by me' – which is a major stumbling-block to many who would like to believe in God but cannot accept that He is a Christian monopoly. I must say that I am among them, and I found another in the Reverend Barney Pityana, an African who serves as a vicar in Milton Keynes:

I have very great difficulties about that. I actually think it is the product of the Church in John's reflective gospel. I'm not persuaded that it is the word of Christ exactly from His lips, and I think it reflects the tradition of a minority that sees itself as a saved community in a world that is very hostile – the beginnings of persecution. I think that at a time when we are a lot more aware of the breadth of the presence of God, of the gifts of God abroad in all people, and that we should be more tolerant in the name of Jesus Christ – that we ought not to confine the grace of God to only those who will affirm a Christ that was never manifested among them for no fault of their own.

New thinking in theology is beginning to concentrate more on Theism and understanding the grounding in God. The saving acts of Jesus Christ are one aspect of the revelation of God, and I think that revelation took other forms. It is hard to accept that, given whole generations of tradition, but I think it is necessary if we are to understand God in His full glory.

I'm bound to feel like this, as an African, because I have always been very concerned about the arrogance of western Christianity crushing the humanity and appropriating everything that was glorious and full and joyful and changing people's lives – all in the name of Jesus Christ and sometimes in very unhappy circumstances. While I myself affirm Christ as a manifestation of God and believe in Him, I'm prepared to grant that there are others, equally valid and equally important. Multi-faith understandings for me are very important.

There will be cries of Heresy! Heresy! And yet I hope Barney Pityana is right, because if he is not there will be few but the strictest of biblical fundamentalists in the Kingdom of Heaven.

One might have thought that if there were a God the least He could have done was to make it clear to us that our life on earth was not the be-all and end-all; that there was an after-life to which we would be admitted according to faith or performance. Many Christians do believe so, and declare it in the creeds; but it has to be admitted that details of that life are sparse and sometimes contradictory – are we to be judged immediately, are we to sleep until the universal Day of Judgment, is there to be a purgatory or nothing but Heaven or Hell? But if there is a God of love and free will, perhaps this is not so surprising. To have the certainty of judgment before us would either be totally paralyzing or would coerce us into a servitude driven by fear rather than love.

This seems to me another way in which God may use doubt, creatively. The fully-believing Christian, pointing to the resurrection of Jesus and the conclusions drawn from it by Paul, may perfectly trust in a life to come; but he cannot *know* what it will be like or what his place will be in it. He can be confident that God is not going to spring some evil trick on him, but he cannot afford to rest on his laurels, either. The closest clue that Jesus gave as to the standards of judgment was whether those to be judged had fed the hungry, clothed the poor and visited the sick and imprisoned, those whom He identified with Himself.

Again and again during this investigation, believers spoke in incarnational terms: that is to say they found God in their fellow human beings. When I asked Ann Semple how she would show God to anyone who asked for Him, she replied:

> I hope this doesn't sound glib, but I would show them a mirror; because I think something the reform churches have missed out on a lot is the idea that God is the breath of life that is in all of us; that He is there to be found. He is not something that we have to seek outside ourselves, in fact. He is there within us, closer than our breathing, closer than the next moment of our life. If you can begin from that point, then you can begin to have a relationship with God.

No doubt the unbeliever will treat this as another last ditch: having failed to find God sitting on a cloud in space, the believers are saying He was really in their heads all the time. At most, Ann Semple is talking about the best in people, another form of Don Cupitt's 'goal that we live by'.

But I am quite sure that was not what she means, and it was not what others meant when they spoke of those moments of illumination or of sensing the presence of God in holy people. It was not a question of being or doing good or better than usual. It was always a sense of loving and being loved in a great at-oneness, as if something within and something without were responding to one another, perfectly synchronized.

Gerry O'Collins, in Rome, spoke of 'the gift of meaning

coming into a situation of absurdity, or a sense of being loved when the situation seems unloving and hateful', and he went on:

> Somehow the light dawns, the penny drops – these are the words people use – and one knows this has happened because they begin to act differently, in ways that are coherent, in ways that show their life has got together in some kind of working order. We all know that when we can't find meaning in things, when things are absurd, we don't know which way to turn. We lack strength, we are without direction and purpose. When people say the light has dawned we see the results of it in their actions or in the strength with which they can endure. The psychologist Victor Frankel has some fine things to say about the concentration camps where meaning was given him through his human and religious experiences; and that allowed him to live and survive where others who found the whole thing totally absurd simply laid down and died. People who don't believe – and many of my friends are non-believers – I certainly wouldn't like to lead that kind of life, in which they don't know where they are going. They can be kindly and so on, but it seems a life in which the light has gone out.

I asked Rowan Williams, in his little Cambridge terrace-house, what difference belief in God made to his life:

> Belief in God grounds my feeling that I can accept what comes to me. I can love and embrace what experience gives me. And I can love myself with my faults, my self-destructiveness, my doubt, uncertainty and deceit. Belief in God, after all, hasn't just got to do with an aesthetic sense. It's also a moral matter – yet not in the sense of imposing demands. It is a moral matter in that the notion of God sets before you a concept of complete truth and transparency which judges, criticizes, irritates and stirs up your own lazy sense of yourself, and at the same time assures you of acceptance, forgiveness, grace and power to go on living. That, to me, is the biggest difference, those two things: a standard of relentless truth, plus forgiveness

and acceptance: that paradox of judgment and mercy which seems to me very central in Christian talk.

So a God who requires us to be absolutely honest about ourselves, but who in return bestows acceptance and healing. Here again is that feeling of 'being known', and it is very much what happens in psychotherapy. This need not upset us, for it does not mean that God is a mere construction of the neurotic. He is rather the very condition of our health. It is the discovery of His presence within us and the alignment of it with His presence in the world around that puts us in a state of grace: that is why the experience is so often described as one of unity. There could be no such unity if God were simply All That Is, for then there would be no separation to be brought together. It is the sense of a separation which can be healed that ultimately persuades me that there is 'something out there' which loves me and to which I must respond with love. I cannot really define it, although the fact that its dominant characteristic *is* love and not power or terror or efficiency seems important; and I believe that we must always be able to interpret experiences of God as something else, or our hand is forced. We are often confused by the fact that God Himself does not stand still: He is on a journey – the dangerous adventure of Creation – and I think the Christian Church has been much too anxious to pin Him down at one time and place in History. Along with Frances Young, I do not think the Bible ties it all up:

> I don't think it is finished and I don't think you can say it is just advances in understanding God, either. There are ups and downs and insights which come at all different levels of the putting together of the Bible . . . We don't get a definitive answer which is going to tie up all the problems. We're invited to accompany God on a pilgrimage, and every one of us has our own pilgrimage in understanding. The intellectual questions are as much a part of it as any other experience we have. I don't think one can separate out those questions from the other levels of understanding or our response to the whole of life.
>
> I don't think, in the end, we are meant to have final answers. I think there is a sense in which the purpose is the

pilgrimage; that now and again we are given glimpses which enable us to move on to the next stage of the pilgrimage. Those glimpses which enable us to feel that after all those years of doubt and wrestling and struggling, suddenly you know that God is real, and you can go on living sure that God is real and that somehow there is hope and that somehow good does come out of evil, because that is what the Cross and the Resurrection are about.

But you go on getting these glimpses. You never see the whole picture. Whether it's an individual or the whole community of the Church, it goes on travelling through history, facing new questions and new circumstances. Now I think the Bible is an important witness to that process in the past and that sometimes its insights, its hints, can actually speak to people across the centuries, and that is what the inspiration of the Bible is all about. The Church has always said it takes the inspiration of the Holy Spirit to *read* the Bible as well as to *form* the Bible. Unless you have the two jelling, then you don't read the Bible in a way that allows the Word of God to speak.

Some will complain there has been far too little about the Bible in this investigation, and I have to admit I have deliberately avoided lengthy reference to it, and for three reasons. First, I think it requires immense scholarship and a knowledge of the original languages which I do not possess. Second, I think it tends to become a closed system of argument that is bound to confirm itself. And third, I wanted to draw upon what people actually feel and believe for themselves today.

Long ago, the case against God was put – and answered – with far greater power than I can muster, in the Book of Job: Job who suffered undeservedly, who catalogued every tribulation of the innocent, who most reasonably protested his righteousness – and got for an answer little more than a magnificent diatribe on the theme 'Who are *you* to criticize God?'

Job caves in and eventually gets his reward. But are we to be so easily satisfied with the answer from the whirlwind? Can we acquit God of cruelty and incompetence?

I think we have learned several things about human suffering in the course of this enquiry. That much of it we are free to inflict upon ourselves, and do so. That much of it we could mitigate or abolish, and fail to do so. That some of it, like death itself, is the inevitable consequence of a universe which seems to be designed with our existence and our freedom in mind. The extraordinarily fine tuning of the basic laws of physics which have allowed our world to come into being may or may not be the work of a Designer and Creator (though the deeper one goes, the more probable it seems that they are); but it is these same laws which are the conditions of our suffering.

We cannot have existence that is worth having, and no suffering; and though we might rather not suffer, there are many things wrong which would not be put right without it. Suffering is often a warning that things are wrong and that they need our attention. To insist that they should not have gone wrong in the first place is to complain that we were born men and women instead of snowflakes or crystals of quartz.

Nevertheless, the real evil of a substantial part of our pain is not to be explained away. With due respect to the oriental faiths, it is not an illusion. I cannot myself believe in the Devil, and have caused great offence among biblical literalists by saying so on the air. *Pace* John Tavener, the Devil has always been a shadowy figure, he is not in the creeds and I think he is in fact *us*, or the way we personify the nastier parts of ourselves without taking the responsibility for them. So suffering is not to be explained away by that device. Suffering is the consequence of the universe as God made it, and He knows it and suffers His own consequences. I find Him guilty of our world but incarnate in it.

If there is a God – a loving God who wills our welfare – the problem of pain, however, cannot be the real crux of the universe. We do wrong to nag at it as if it were. Christians would say the real point of Christ is not the Crucifixion but the Resurrection – not the squalid torment but its glorious trans- formation into life. Whether it is a myth-story or a historical but supernatural fact, the essence of it is the same: the demonstra- tion that there is That of God in Every One which can overcome the evil in the world, whether it be violence, pain or malevo- lence. This *That* is not a magic ray beamed down from outer space. It is enfleshed, incarnate in mankind: the Son of Man

(Daughter if you will) who is also Son of God. That of God is Love; not to be understood sentimentally but as a deep caring, a grasping for unity, which penetrates even the deepest suffering. But it is not actually about suffering, which it wears almost as a disguise to stimulate and provoke us: it is about creation and healing and joy.

Personally I do believe that Christianity (whose images I use instinctively) is the most beautifully developed and, for me, the truest way of understanding God. But I think the time is upon us when Christians must look with respect at other great religions and realise that God has been at work in them, too. God may appear fuzzy to us as we try to take in the whole spectrum of faiths, but to any one of them He is quite sharply in focus. They have not been looking at the wrong objective, but each has been focusing from a different point of view.

Frankly, I cannot believe that God cares very much what we believe about Him in detail: whether we have got the relationships in the Trinity right, whether we are sound on the significance of the Eucharist, whether we truly affirm the Virgin Birth and the Empty Tomb. These things are surely our loss or gain, not His. What I think matters is whether we hear Him and how we respond to Him, and I think there are plenty of unbelievers who do both admirably without putting His name to them, for He has this reluctance to go around fixing His official stamp on things. From His point of view there is no distinction between the world and God's World; there is only the one world which we are free to recognise as His or not.

So belief in God remains optional, and the sentence that He suffers for being guilty of the world but Incarnate is an eternity of being at our mercy. Were it not for the world of men, His Love would be like an egg unfertilized: perfect but sterile. What a fix He has got Himself in! What power we hold over Him! What dangerous adventure!

What a preposterous God, you may say. Either this is the purest subjective fiction or else the most blasphemous heresy, for surely it is man who is on trial and the inevitable sentence for all of us is death (with possibly worse to come). But the God I am hinting at is, literally, the God of Love: yearning, vulnerable, capable of all things if only touched off by Love. That such a

188 The Case Against God

being is worthy of our love may be reckoned in the head; but the
desire to do so can only come from the heart.

My interview with Michael Dummett (*Chapter Four*) was, for
the most part, very much an exercise of the head. It was only at
the end that I asked him why, personally and not as a philosopher, he believed in God; and he opened up his heart:

> I have reasons for belief in God which I tried to gesture at
> in some of the things I have said. But such reasons can be
> very powerful at one moment and at another can look very
> flimsy. One can wonder if one's whole thinking hasn't
> gone awry, and whether you can rest anything on such
> very general reflections. I will take your question as asking
> me why this is something I have to hang on to; and I do feel
> exactly that. I of course have moments when I do feel it is a
> question of hanging on. I think it is a matter of keeping
> faith with certain perceptions, certain ideals which I have
> given my faith to – in the sense of loyalty.

Somewhat rudely, I asked if he meant that he did not want to
let himself down? Speaking humbly and with great effort,
Professor Dummett went on:

> No, it isn't that. I suppose in what I said about morality I
> might have sounded as though I was giving Mount Sinai as
> the picture of believing in God. But the most important
> thing is that it makes sense to talk about doing things for
> the *love* of God. Now, it is presumptuous of me to mention
> such things, but the fact is that the few lives that exemplify
> something far above the average (as the rather frequent
> example of human wickedness are the lowest) are the lives
> that are devoted to the love of God. For the love of God
> people do what, from any other standpoint, is throwing
> away their lives. I'm not talking only about people who
> risk martyrdom but who give up their whole lives to
> relieving the suffering of the utterly wretched, or for that
> matter those who give their lives to penance and contem-
> plation. I don't know anywhere else we can find anything
> that counterbalances the extremes of human wickedness
> which very frequently occur. The one thing I feel I cannot
> do is to adopt a view of the world which would make

nonsense of such lives. When it comes to it, that is where my loyalty lies.

In the end it is the Communion of Saints that convinces us that God exists.

And so, in a final pilgrimage, I took my stand upon Holy Island, off the Northumberland coast, among the windblasted remains of the priory where St Aidan and St Cuthbert prayed and where men and women still come for holiness as they have done for fourteen hundred years; not because of magic or superstition (the faithful are not really such idiots) but because, when they looked for Him and did not just argue about Him, God was there and made sense. But we must never think we can capture Him or put walls and a roof around Him, as the Church has tried to do time and again. Eventually, every attempt to imprison Him collapses, and the gales of God sweep on through the ruins.

Witnesses Interviewed

Dr Zahira Abdin
Jane Adams
Alison Adcock
Karen Armstrong
Uri Avneri
Professor Sir Alfred Ayer
Sister Therese Mary Barnett
Rev Douglas Bean
Dr David Bellamy
Rev Downing Berners-Wilson
Rt Rev Stuart Blanch
Dr Meg Booth
Professor John Bowker
Dr Margaret Bowker
Deaconess Shelagh Brown
Professor Owen Chadwick
P. C. Chatterji
Gerry Cohen
Dr Ian Cohen
Rev Don Cupitt
Lord Dacre of Glanton
Professor Paul Davies
Father Marcel Dubois
Professor Michael Dummett
Gai Eaton
Mohammed Sherif El-Herrawi
Ronald Eyre
Father Michel Farrell
Hilary Field
Lord Fitt
Dr Michael Goulder
Rabbi Hugo Gryn
Bishop Michael Hare-Duke
Rev Richard Harries
David Hay
Paul Heelas
Dr James Hemming
Roger Hooker
Michael Jones
Margaret Kane
Dr Ze'ev Katz

Patrick J. Kavanagh
David Keddie
Robert King-Edward
His Holiness the Dalai Lama
Marghanita Laski
Rabbi Alan Levine
Alastair McDonald
Sister Monica Meehan
Father Tom Michel
Dr Jonathan Miller
John Mortimer
Iris Murdoch
Dr Ashish Nandi
Rabbi Julia Neuberger
Donald Nicholls
Monsignor Jack O'Brien
Father Gerry O'Collins
Gillian Orde
Bernard Ossen
Father Rex Pai
Penina Peli
Barney Pityana
Professor John Polkinghorne
Sheikh Abdullah Schleifer
John Selwyn Gummer
Ann Semple
Father Michael Sharkey
Dr Rupert Sheldrake
Ethel Snowball
Professor Richard Swinburne
Monsignor Dick Stewart
John Tavener
Bishop John V. Taylor
Salma Valjgi
Professor Keith Ward
Professor Zwi Werblowski
Canon Rowan Williams
Shirley Williams
David Winter
Dr Frances Young

Bibliography

ARMSTRONG, Karen *Beginning the World* Macmillan 1983

AYER, A. J. *The Central Questions of Philosophy* Weidenfeld 1973

BEARDSWORTH, T. *A Sense of Presence* Religious Experience Unit (Oxford) 1977

BERKELEY, G. *Principles of Human Knowledge* (many editions)

BOWKER, J. *Worlds of Faith* Ariel Books (BBC) 1983

COLVER, A. W. & PRICE, J. V. *David Hume on Religion* OUP 1976

CUPITT, Don *Taking Leave of God* SCM 1980

CUPITT, Don *The World to Come* SCM 1982

DAVIES, Paul *God and the New Physics* Dent 1983

DOCTRINE COMMISSION of the Church of England *Christian Believing* SPCK 1976

DOSTOEVSKY *The Idiot* Penguin Classics 1955

FEUERBACH, L. *The Essence of Christianity* Kegan Paul 1893

FREUD, S. *Totem and Taboo. The Future of an Illusion* Hogarth 1957 & 1961

GOULDER, M. & HICK, J. *Why Believe in God?* SCM 1983

HARDY, Alister *The Spiritual Nature of Man* Clarendon 1979

HICK, J. (editor) *The Myth of God Incarnate* SCM 1977

ISRAEL, Martin *The Pain that Heals (The place of suffering)* Hodder 1981

JAMES, William *The Varieties of Religious Experience* Fount 1981

JUNG, C. G. *Psychology and Religion* Routledge (collected works) 1960

KÜNG, Hans *Does God Exist?* (The major study of the subject) Collins 1980

LEWIS, C. S. *God in the Dock* Fount 1982

MACKIE, J. L. *The Miracle of Theism* Oxford 1982

MARX, Karl *Contribution to the Critique of Hegel's Philosophy of Law* 1844

MITCHELL, B. *The Justification of Religious Belief* Macmillan 1973

MURDOCH, Iris *The Sovereignty of Good* Routledge 1970

NIETZSCHE, Friedrich *Twilight of the Idols; The Anti-Christ* Penguin Classics 1972

SHELDRAKE, Rupert *A New Science of Life* Paladin/Granada 1983

SWINBURNE, Richard *The Coherence of Theism* Oxford 1977

SWINBURNE, Richard *The Existence of God* Oxford 1981

TOYNBEE, Philip *Towards the Holy Spirit* SCM 1982
WARD, Keith *Holding Fast to God* SPCK 1982